*The Wal… Series*

# THE P… RICT
## *White … land*

### *In…oduction*

The Peak District is a beautiful oasis almost entirely surrounded by large industrial towns which in 1951 was designated a National Park. It is comprised of parts of six counties - Cheshire, Derbyshire, Greater Manchester, Staffordshire, South Yorkshire and West Yorkshire. It is a rare mix of bleak moorland, peat bogs, limestone crags and green pastures bounded by drystone walls.

Despite its name The Peak contains no high mountains. It comes from the Saxon word for 'hill'. It is rugged walking country, well garnished with small towns and villages, crags to climb, sparkling trout streams to fish and historical buildings and gardens to visit. The Peak District is split into two roughly equal halves, the White in the south and the Dark in the north.

The White Peak takes its name from its limestone bedrock. It is a tableland of buttresses. Of these the most spectacular is Dovedale, but others like Monsal Dale, Lathkill Dale and the Manifold Valley also deserve exploration on foot as do others too narrow for roads. It was a centre for lead mining from Roman times until the C19th, industry and farming living together down the centuries.

Bakewell, famed for its pudding and tarts, is the only town of any size in the White Peak. Its museum houses a fine collection of country exhibits. Matlock Bath, in a narrow part of the Derwent Valley, has a cable-car ride to the Heights of Abraham, where the Great Rutland Cavern, a restored C17th lead mine in working order is found.

The old custom of 'Well Dressing' is carried out in many White Peak towns and villages during the summer months, participants going to great lengths to design pictures, usually on a religious theme, from flower petals. Once completed, these pictures stand along side the wells for a week or more and have become a major tourist attraction.

Magnificent Chatsworth, home of the Dukes of Devonshire, sited near the River Derwent in glorious parkland, is the most famous historical building in the White Peak, with Haddon Hall, a rambling C14th manor house, with its terraced rose garden, a close second.

The Dark Peak, which covers the northern half of the National Park, thrusts two arms into the White Peak in an embrace. The bedrock from which it gets its name is Millstone Grit, which produces a landscape dominated by rounded hills capped with peat bogs from which run drainage channels or groughs.

Kinder Scout, at 622 metres (2,038ft), is the highest point in the Peak and Bleaklow and Black Hill mirror the harshness. The Upper Derwent Valley and the Goyt Valley, with their reservoirs, show its gentler face.

Buxton in the Dark Peak but just outside the National Park, is the highest spa town in England. Poole's Cavern is at Buxton. Caves are the Dark Peak's main attraction. Others include the Peak Cavern, Bagshaw Cavern and Blue John Cavern.

Lyme Hall, a fine Palladian mansion with a large deer park, is, perhaps, the Dark Peak's most famous historical building.

Together the White Peak and the Dark Peak become an area of considerable variety giving the Peak District perhaps more than its fair share of beautiful countryside. And you, dear reader, are the one who reaps the benefit.

*The famous panoramic viewpoint of Monsal Head Viaduct*

# The Grouse Inn
## Longshaw

It is astonishing to realise that less than five miles south of industrial Sheffield you can relax in the unspoiled natural beauty of the Longshaw Estate, one thousand and five hundred acres of open moorland, plantations and grazing land that includes the lovely Padley Gorge, which is clothed with ancient woodland. The estate was purchased from the Duke of Rutland by public subscription and given to the National Trust when he sold his estate in 1927.

*Where to find us*

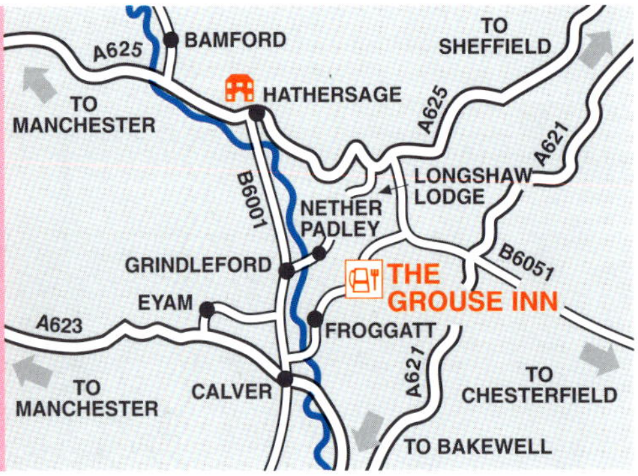


Near the edge of the gritstone Dark Peak there are several curious rock formations, one of which is the Rocking Stone, a huge boulder that balances precariously on a group of rocks in Lawrence Field not far from the stark remains of an ancient village.

This is gritstone country and many abandoned millstones and gritstones are scattered along the gritstone edges above the Derwent Valley. There are hundreds of them near Longshaw, below Surprise View, many stacked, half-buried, alongside the route of an old tramway.

The gritstone edges along the eastern side of the River Derwent are a prominent geographical feature and from the paths that run along the tops of most of them there are spectacular views. Of these edges the most outstanding are Birchen Edge, Gardom's Edge, Baslow Edge, Curbar Edge, Froggatt Edge, Millstone Edge, Burbage Edge and Stanage Edge. Many are popular with rock climber's and on two of them there are monuments. Nelson's Monument was erected on Birchen Edge by a local man in 1810. It stands close to three large rocks that look like ships. They are named 'Victory', 'Defiant' and 'Royal Soverin'. The monument on Baslow Edge was erected in 1866 for Wellington.

Below the gritstone edges, in the valley bottom, lies the village of Calver close to where, on the steep hillside, is famous Cliff College, headquarters of the methodist Ministry. Whenever Billy Graham visits England he stays at Cliff College and people in their thousands flock to hear him preach.

A former cotton mill at Calver, used in the TV series 'Colditz', was built in 1803-4 by Richard Arkright.

The Grouse Inn is older than that. It was built towards the end of the C17th. It is a friendly pub, set in six acres, and from it there are some glorious views. It has a patio, log fires and two bars.

There is a good choice of liquid refreshment: Wards' Bitter, Vaux Extra Special, Waggledance and Guinness. Carlsberg and Labatts, Strongbow cider and various bottled beers, lagers and ciders are also on offer. Over and above the usual shorts and spirits there are forty-five different malt whiskies.

Bar meals and traditional Sunday lunches are available. Meals are served Lunchtime and evening all week except Monday and Tuesday evenings and vegetarians are catered for. There are spicy meals, mixed grills, steak and kidney pies, salads and sandwiches.

The Grouse Inn serves from 12 noon until 2.30pm daily and from 7pm until 9.30pm in the evenings. The bar is open 12 noon until 3pm and 6pm until 11pm.

**<u>For further information, contact:</u>**

**THE GROUSE INN,**
**LONGSHAW,**
**SHEFFIELD,**
**DERBYSHIRE, S11 7TZ**
**TEL: 01433 630423**

# Crich Pottery

## Crich

Crich has overlooked the Derwent Valley since Roman times. The name means 'place on the hill' and some two thousand rural folk live there. Perhaps it is their endearing traits and gentle eccentricity coupled with the beautiful local topography of this pretty farming landscape that decided the television people to use it as the setting for 'Peak Practice', a popular drama about a country medical practice.

There is a disused limestone quarry above the village and a National Tramway Museum in it. The forty trams it contains were all built between 1873 and 1953. It also has a reconstructed C19th street and scenic tram rides are available.

At Crich Pottery, in Crich Market Place, there is a rich heritage to be discovered as well. The Pottery buildings had been in farming use until they were converted to their current function in 1974. However, the Gallery was restored much more recently in 1992 and has a long history. They were originally constructed sometime around 1670 to 1700 as cottages for farm workers but eventually fell into dereliction some 30 years ago.

Today, Crich Pottery enjoys a tremendous setting of farm buildings surrounding a courtyard where can be found the Pottery Workshop, Gallery with Coffee Shop and 'Seconds' Shop upstairs above it, and Stables.

Diana Worthy was Royal College of Art trained and is owner and partner with David Worthy, and the thrower, Ian Harris, was trained at Loughborough College of Art. Throwing is the process of shaping the clay on the potter's wheel and is a very skilled occupation. The Potter works with clays and clay bodies and at Crich Pottery their splendid specialisation is in stoneware.

There is something magical about the effect of clay and fire, in which mud is transformed into an object of art. Little wonder that the ancient Chinese set great store by their ceramic creations. The transformation of clay into a thing of beauty is not easily attained. It hides behind a mass of technical jargon which must be studied and digested or by-passed.

Forming clay and creating from it something that has form and beauty is deeply satisfying to the spirit and pleasing to the eye.

Whilst exploring the Peak District and enjoying the craftsmanship displayed in the Pottery and Gallery, what better place could there be to partake of some refreshment. Available daily between 10am and 6pm are tea, coffee, and juice along with the tasty and mouth-watering delights such as flapjack, carrot cake and muffins that are supplied by the Handmade Flapjack Company.

Visitors frequently praise the high quality objects made at Crich Pottery and created in the fertile mind and capable hands of Diana, David, Ian and their helpers. Indeed, their carefully crafted products provide as much inspiration and enjoyment for the visitor as the beautiful countryside of woodland and fields that makes this such wonderful walking country. All things considered, this is a magical place to visit.

*Where to find us*

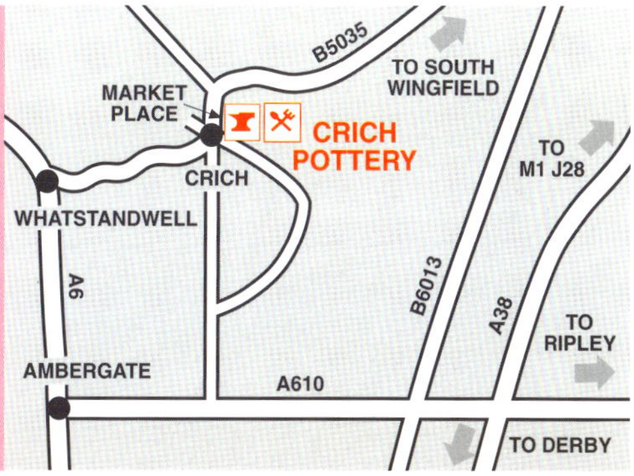


**For further information, contact:**

**CRICH POTTERY,
MARKET PLACE, CRICH,
DERBYSHIRE, DE4 5DD
TEL: 01773 853171
FAX: 01773 857325**

# Eyam Hall
## Eyam

Eyam is a picturesque village nestling among hills at the junction of the White Peak and the Dark Peak. A village has occupied this site since Saxon times, the wild, heather covered gritstone moors rising above it, the dramatic cave-riddled limestone cliffs of Eyam Dale and Middleton Dale below.

Where to find us

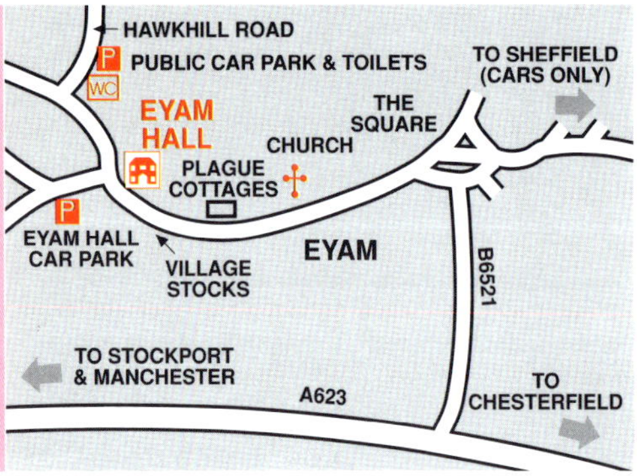


The village is best known for the bravery of its inhabitants when faced with the plague in 1665-6. The germs, carried by rat fleas, arrived in Eyam in a box of cloth delivered to the village tailor. George Viccars was bitten by a flea as he unpacked the cloth. He died a few days later. The disease quickly spread, yet, despite their fear of it, the villagers decided to remain where they were rather than risk spreading the disease by fleeing to safety. The plague claimed the lives of 260 villagers, many of them young children. Plague Cottage, where this frightful outbreak started, can still be seen.

Eyam Hall was built in 1671-2 by Thomas Wright of Unthank for his son, John. The Wright family were Derbyshire gentry whose money came from lead mining. John married a local heiress, Elizabeth Kniveton, who had a considerable say in the design of Eyam Hall, their future home. Their descendants have always lived there, each generation adding furniture, portraits and objects of interest. To Robert and Nicola Wright Eyam Hall is still very much their home today. It is friendly and welcoming and the rooms are homely and intimate.

The Buttery is located in the Hall's original outbuildings and the Wrights believe that it serves the best range of cakes in Derbyshire. The ever popular Granny Sampson's Sticky Toffee Teabread is amazingly moist and rich; perhaps the most delicious tea bread you have ever tasted. Also available are an especially large, rich, chocolate gateau, cream cakes, pavlova, fruit tarts and delicious sponges and scones which melt in the mouth.

Food is cooked daily on the premises, only the best fresh ingredients being used. The menu varies daily, there being two or three hot dishes with a vegetarian option. Particular favourites include spinakopita, a delicious Greek dish, and Tudor Pie, a delightfully creamy concoction made with chicken and apricot from a secret recipe. Quiche is available in a variety of enticing and unusual flavours like broccoli and blue cheese, Stilton and walnut or asparagus.

Drinks include speciality and herb teas; freshly made filter coffee; delicious, unusual, fruit-flavoured mineral waters, home-made lemon squash with lemon rind and an unbeatable flavour; canned drinks and hot chocolate with lashings of whipped cream.

The Hall is open from the beginning of April until the end of October, Wednesdays, Thursdays, Sundays and Bank Holiday Mondays from 11am. Last tour 4.30pm.

The Buttery is open weekends in March, 10.30am to 5pm. From from the beginning of April until the end of October, every day except Monday; and Bank Holiday Mondays, 10.30am to 5.30pm.

Both Hall and Buttery may be visited by booked parties outside normal hours by prior arrangement.

**For further information, contact:**

**EYAM HALL,**
**EYAM,**
**SHEFFIELD, S30 1QW**
**TEL: 01433 631976**
**FAX: 01433 631976**

# The Rising Sun Hotel

## Castleton Road, Bamford

Bamford has a cotton mill which was built circa 1792. It has a large water wheel and a 1907 tandem-compound steam engine. Each year there are open days when the engine is run under steam.

Hope has an ancient church with an unusual C14th broach spire. There is a Saxon cross shaft in the churchyard. There are two fonts in the church, one C12th, the other dated 1662. The latter was brought from Derwent church when it was demolished to make way for Ladybower Reservoir. The twin hills of Lose Hill and Win Hill are behind the village and the River Noe flows between them to join the Peakshole Water at Hope village.

Between Bamford and Hope is The Rising Sun Hotel, an old coaching house built around 1700. Set in one and a half acres of gardens, it has parking facilities for sixty cars and two coaches. There is an informal bar inside, a family room and a dining area.

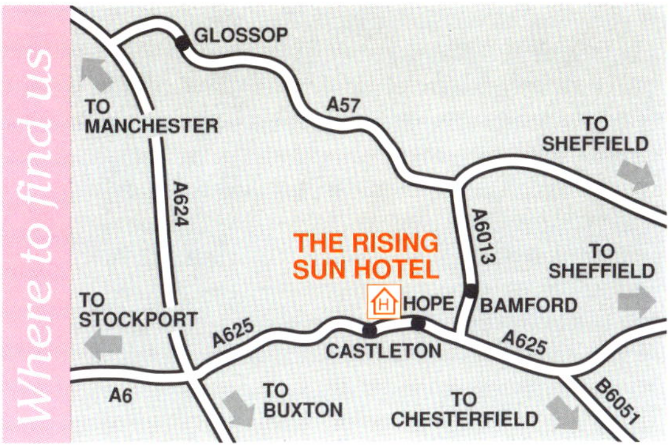


The full stocked bar includes three real ales and wine lists. Bar meals are served from 12 noon until 9pm.

Morning coffee at The Rising Sun Hotel makes an excellent start to an exploration of this tranquil area. Perhaps a walk along the narrow valley of the River Noe northwards for a couple of pleasant miles to where, in the Vale of Edale, the valley widens and turns westwards. There at the foot of Edale Moor, is tiny Edale village, the southern end of the Pennine Way. The ridge that runs along the southern side of the valley makes an exhilarating alternative walk. From Lose Hill at its eastern end to Mam Tor there are spectacular views on either side. It is a fine introduction to the Dark Peak.

Maybe pony trekking across the high ground above Ladybower Reservoir is more to your liking, or a splendid walk around it, partly on high ground, in part close to the reservoir's edge.

The dam at the northern, top end of Ladybower Reservoir holds back Derwent Reservoir which, in turn, holds back Howden Reservoir into which the River Derwent flows from the bleak Howden Moors. The Derwent is the major river of the Dark Peak and the building of the Derwent reservoirs had a profound effect on the upper valley.

Work on Howden Dam began in 1901 and on Derwent Dam a year later. Howden was completed in 1912 and Derwent in 1916. During their construction two villages, Derwent and Ashopton were flooded by the waters of Ladybower Reservoir.

During World War II the RAF's 617 squadron used Derwent Reservoir for practice runs before the famous Dambusters raid on Germany.

There are many other interesting attractions within close proximity to the The Rising Sun Hotel where a hearty meal can bring a day's adventure to a happy climax.

A selection of the chef's specials include Chilli Con Carni, Roast of the Day, Chicken à la Creme, Mushroom Stroganoff, Steak Diane and Pork Normandie. There is a children's menu; and a carvery lunch every Sunday.

**For further information, contact:**

**THE RISING SUN HOTEL,
CASTLETON ROAD,
BAMFORD, SHEFFIELD,
DERBYSHIRE, S30 2AL
TEL: 01433 651323 FAX: 01433 651601**

# Scotland Nurseries

## Tansley, Matlock

The name Tansley means 'a valley branching from a main dale' and its strongest claim to fame is its situation, rather than its size. It is this fact, precisely, that has been of great benefit to many discerning people visiting this beautiful part of the Peak District.

Where to find us

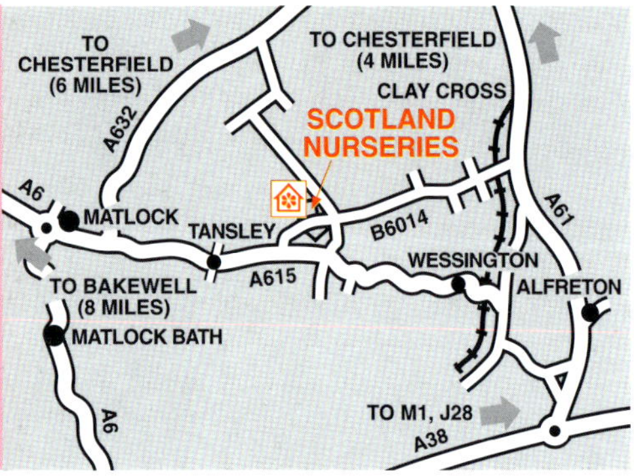


Matlock and Matlock Bath, less than three miles away are both great attractions with much to offer. Beneath the 'Heights of Abraham' there is a restored C17th lead mine. It is in working order and guided tours into it are a popular feature. A cable car ride up or down this steep sided part of the Derwent valley is a great thrill and not to be missed; and the views across the surrounding countryside are terrific.

It is from the old spa hotel buildings in Matlock that Derbyshire is administered, a convenient arrangement because Matlock, or thereabouts, is where the midlands end and the north begins, where productive corn fields give way to higher, grassy pastures, bounded by dry stone walls and where the accents of the local's change.

Chatsworth, the magnificent home of the Dukes of Devonshire, set in glorious parkland, near the River Derwent, is only five miles distant. This most palatial of England's great country houses was probably designed by Thomas Archer, aided by the Duke of Devonshire. It carries the Cavendish family arms over the pediment.

The most romantic of Elizabethan buildings, Haddon Hall, near Bakewell, is also only 5 miles away from Tansley. It was there that Sir George Vernon entertained so lavishly during the C16th that he became known as the 'King of the Peak'.

These and other attractions, all part of the infinite variety of the Peak District, make happy memories and souvenirs of a visit are always in great demand. But what forms should they take? Something from Matlock, Chatsworth or Haddon Hall perhaps or something to represent the area as a whole?

If the latter, Scotland Nurseries, at Tansley, has the answer. Set in forty-five acres of delightful Derbyshire countryside, the Garden Centre has a craft shop, discount clothing store, children's play room and coffee shop. This is the place to come to for your souvenirs. The garden shop and craft area is pleasantly set within a tastefully converted Victorian barn and the coffee shop will sustain you while you decide on your purchase.

Open seven days a week from 9am until 5pm, this Egon Ronay recommended establishment serves morning coffee, lunches and afternoon teas. Be it just tea, coffee or soft drinks or something more substantial, the same high standard of personal service is maintained. All is home-baked and there is a good variety: soups quiches, salads, lasagnes and pies being among the foods always available.

For anyone taking a peek at the eastern side of the Peak let Scotland Nurseries help you select a suitable memento, one that will grow as strongly as your love of this fascinating area is sure to once you have seen it.

**For further information, contact:**

**SCOTLAND NURSERIES,**
**TANSLEY, MATLOCK,**
**DERBYSHIRE, DE4 5GT**
**TEL: 01629 583036**
**FAX: 01629 583013**

# Ye Olde Cheshire Cheese Inn

## Castleton

Castleton takes its name from the castle which has stood on the edge of the limestone cliff for nine hundred years. William the Conqueror's bastard son William Peveril built it in 1086.

The keep was added by Henry II in 1176. For two hundred years it was one of the strongest fortresses in Derbyshire, commanding the western entrance to the Hope Valley, as it still does. Ruinous since the C17th, most of its imposing grandeur remains. It inspired Sir Walter Scott to write 'Peveril of The Peak'.

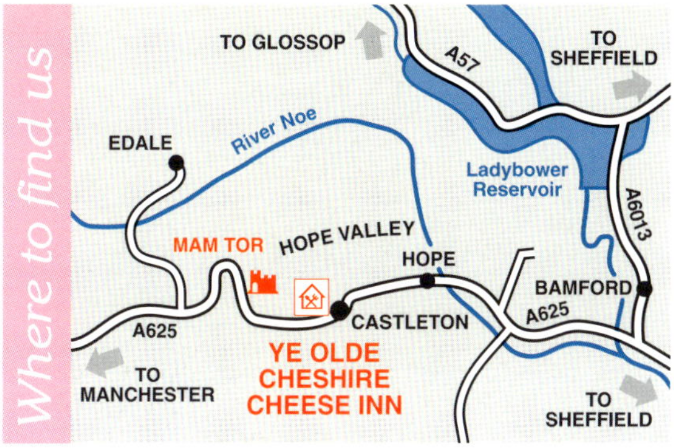


Soon after the castle was built, so was the village. Its church, St Edmund's, is mostly Norman, though much was restored and rebuilt in the early 1800s. Many of the solid, limestone houses are C18th. Castleton lies in the middle of that part of the Peak District National Park famed for its limestone caves.

The largest one, Peak Cavern, is at the bottom of the cliff on which the castle stands. Its entrance, sixty feet high and twice as wide, is thought to be the largest of any in Britain. For more than five hundred years rope-makers used the cave and some of them lived in cottages inside the cave entrance. The cottages have gone, but the rope walks remain.

Speedwell, Treak Cliff and Blue John are three other caves close to Castleton. All are noted for their banded veins of blue, yellow and red mineral known as Blue John, which has been used for making jewellery and ornaments since Roman times.

One of the finest walks in the Peak District begins about two miles west of Castleton. It is the two and a half miles long ridge walk from Mam Tor to Lose Hill. Because of landslips on Mam Tor's eastern side caused by unstable strata in the rock, it is called the 'Shivering Mountain'. The views from its summit and along the ridge walk are fantastic.

Ye Olde Cheshire Cheese Inn is a family run, C17th, free house, sited in Castleton, and infused with the atmosphere of yesteryear by caring proprietors, Ken and Angie Slack. There are no machines, no pool tables and no juke box, and this enhances the restfulness of gentler times. Good home-cooking, good ale and good company are assured. All of which allows guests to feel snug and secure, enabling them to relax completely.

There are two heavily beamed traditional lounge bars, cosy seating in four luxuriously carpeted lounges, a roaring fire and full central heating. The six bedrooms are prettily decorated with en-suite, colour TV, tea, coffee and hair dryers.

A unique mouth watering menu includes roast wild boar, game pie, pheasant, smoked chicken and home-made pies. There are over thirty home-made dishes from which to choose.

If pampering is what you seek, look no further than Ye Olde Cheshire Cheese Inn where yesterday's milieu is still alive today.

**For further information, contact:**

**YE OLDE CHESHIRE CHEESE INN,
HOW LANE, CASTLETON,
SHEFFIELD, DERBYSHIRE
S30 2WJ
TEL: 01433 620330**

# The Pool Café & Tea Rooms

## Hathersage

Hathersage lies on a hillside above the Hope Valley sheltered by the long low gritstone cliffs of Millstone Edge and Stanage Edge.

Its ancient Church of St Michael built in 1381, was enlarged in the C15th and restored in 1851. It overlooks the village and its decorated spire is a landmark in the valley. One of Robin Hood's merry men, Little John, was born in Hathersage.

He made his living as a nailer before joining the outlaw's band. He is buried in St Michael's churchyard. You can't miss the grave. Surrounded by neat railings, it lies alongside the path and is fourteen feet long.

Across the road from the churchyard entrance is C15th Highbury Cottage, the oldest in the village. The stone tower on the opposite hillside once used to house hunting dogs. The ditch and mound behind Highbury Cottage is thought to be either a Saxon earthworks or a Norman motte and bailey castle.

Charlotte Brontë based her 'Norton' in 'Jane Eyre' on Hathersage. She visited the C18th vicarage and her 'Moor House' in the novel is probably Moorseats Hall, which can be seen behind the vicarage. The novelist probably took the name 'Eyre' from the Derbyshire family who have monuments in St Michael's church. Robert Eyre is said to have built houses for each of his seven sons during the C16th. Five of them, including Hathersage Hall and one and a half miles distant North Lees Hall still survives.

An important village industry was wire drawing, a process in needle making. The industry was housed in Dale Mill in Dale Road, which was built in the 1700s.

Visitors to Hathersage will find sustenance and refreshment at The Pool Café and Tea Rooms. It was built in 1935 and has been used as a school canteen and dining hall and for workers building the Ladybower and Derwent dams. Perhaps this link inspired the owners to build an adjoining open air swimming pool. It is heated to eighty-five degrees centigrade and is open Monday to Saturday from the end of April until mid-September. Non-swimmers can use the tennis courts and bowling green.

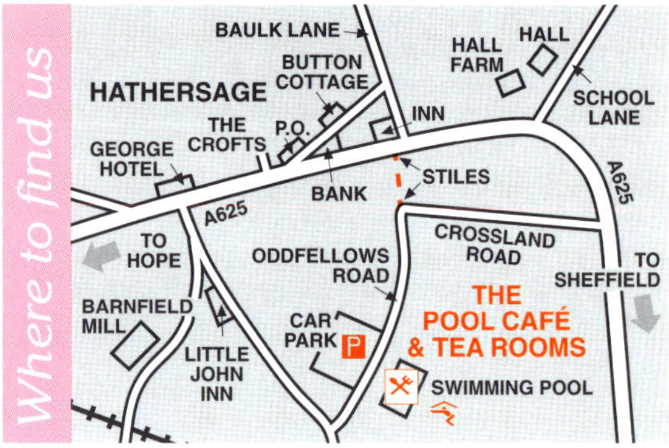


Umbrellas sprouting like multi-coloured mushrooms on the lawn area outside the café shade those dining under the open sky. Inside there is seating for forty-two people and a nearby play area for children.

The Pool Café is open seven days a week from the end of April until the end of September and on Thursdays, Fridays, Saturdays and Sundays throughout the winter months for morning coffee, breakfasts, snacks, lunches, afternoon teas, cream teas and the consumption of home-made cakes and other pleasurable pastimes. Thursdays, Fridays and Saturdays are also fish and chip take-away days, for which the café is widely noted. A full menu is served throughout the year and booking is advised for December lunches. Specialities of the house include 'Hikers' Hash', a wholesome meal served in a bowl or in a large Yorkshire Pudding.

Coach parties are also welcome by prior booking.

**For further information, contact:**

**THE POOL CAFÉ & TEA ROOMS,<br>ODDFELLOWS ROAD,<br>HATHERSAGE,<br>DERBYSHIRE, S30 1BL<br>TEL: 01433 651159**

# Poppies
## Tideswell

For the most part the names of villages fall into clearly defined categories and Tideswell is no exception. It refers to an early owner of a stream 'Tidi's Stream', and is mentioned in the Domesday Book. Like so many of our villages, Tideswell owes its charm to chance, the result of centuries of unplanned and undisciplined growth. Clustering around the original nucleus of the parish church, the village community grew. A cottage was built here, a village shop there; and as it developed the need for such communal buildings as a school, an inn and a village hall became a necessity. So developed a pleasing jumble of variety between individual buildings and in Tideswell the structures as a whole blended to give the village its own look because of the general use of the local Derbyshire stone.

At one time Tideswell was the fifth largest place in Derbyshire. In 1993 it was nominated the best kept Derbyshire village and the following year it won the East Midlands Region of the Britain in Bloom award. Both are wonderful achievements of which the inhabitants are justifiably proud.

None are prouder than David and Valerie Pinnegar whose restaurant, Poppies, is situated right in the middle of this lovely village in what had once been the village store.

The restaurant's main dining room seats up to thirty, the tea room covers fifteen and a high chair is available. It is licensed and serves wines, spirits and beer in cans. Soft drinks and mineral water are also obtainable.

During the summer Poppies is open on Mondays, Tuesdays and Fridays between 10.30am and 4.30pm and from 7pm until 9.30pm. On Saturdays it is 9.30am until 5pm and 7pm until 9.30pm. Sundays it is open from 12 noon until 7.30pm. It is closed Wednesdays and Thursdays. During the winter months it is open on Fridays and Saturdays as during the summer and on Sundays from 12 noon until 5pm.

Valerie does most of the cooking. A pot of Earl Grey is the perfect accompaniment to her home-made cakes, cream and fruit teas with Lapsang Souchong and Darjeeling among the alternatives. There are also fruit and herbal teas for the adventurous and the coffee comes filtered or decaffeinated.

Snacks range from home-made soup to stir fry vegetables with meat, salads include various cheeses and prawn and the sandwiches have a multitude of fillings.

A choice of seven starters like a Two Salmon Pasta and Spanakopita give a wonderful start to the à la carte evening meals, half of which are vegetarian dishes. The Smoky Lamb and Boeuf au vin are excellent as are the Vegetarian Medley and the Chestnut, Sage and Red Wine Loaf. To round off the meal there are desserts from Poppies home-made selection, Bradwell's ice cream or the cheese platter with coffee.

After a day looking round Chatsworth or walking, climbing or caving in the locality, cap it with a perfect finalé, an excellent evening meal at Poppies.

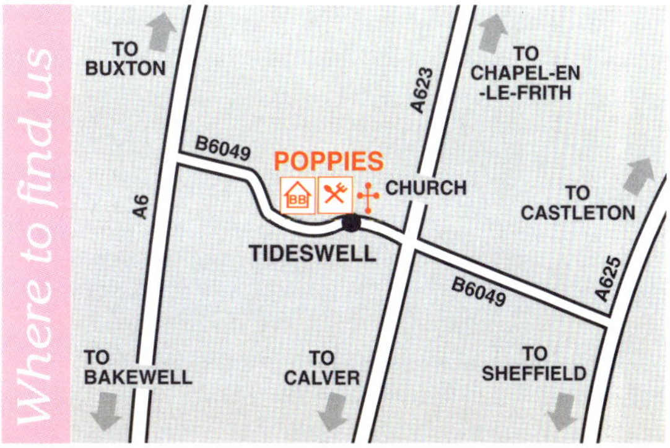


**For further information, contact:**

**POPPIES,**
**BANK SQUARE, TIDESWELL,**
**BUXTON, DERBYSHIRE,**
**SK17 8LA**
**TEL: 01298 871083**

# Toto's Coffee House & Bistro

## Glossop

Glossop, 'Glott's hop or valley' is related to 'glotzen', to stare, and means 'the valley of staring men', probably because of all the stone heads with staring eyes found thereabouts. It is sited where the A57 from Sheffield, over the Snake Pass, meets the A624 which runs northwards from Hayfield.

Coombes Edge, rising to the west, marks the western boundary of the Peak District at this point. Glossop developed as a textile town in the C19th, but as the town's Heritage Centre shows its history goes back ten thousand years.

Toto's Coffee House and Bistro, formerly a hotel which the proprietors Janet Husband and Nicholas Healey, opened in 1993 having transformed the washroom basement into a Mediterranean Oasis.

Flag floors, beamed ceilings, white-washed walls and more than a hint of Mediterranean flair and music immerse patrons in an aura reminiscent of sangria and sun. To help soak up the sunshiny atmosphere there is a full range of alcoholic and soft drinks, coffee and tea.

The palms that wave at Toto's Coffee House and Bistro are attached to hands and impart 'welcome' from Tuesday to Saturday between 10.30am and 4.30pm; and after siesta Thursday, Friday and Saturday 7pm until last orders at 10pm.

Be it a cup of coffee you require, a snack or a full meal, Toto's Coffee House and Bistro can cater for your needs. Their morning coffee can imbrue a customer with a glow warm enough to counter a cool Derbyshire day, and the extensive lunches and evening meals, where all the food is freshly prepared.

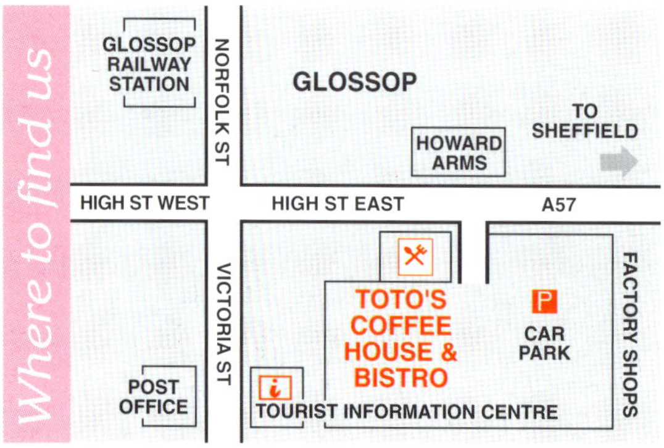


Toto's Coffee House and Bistro is nothing if not Cosmopolitan: there is a wide range of Mediterranean, South American and English dishes. So, if like England's Big Ben, you have the time, and like Italy's leaning tower, you have the inclination, try a South American steak and Spanish onions with French fries.

Should you wish to see the northern moors without too much effort take the A57 from Glossop for four miles to where on Featherbed Moss, there is a Pennine Way sign. From here, walk northwards, following a line of posts, soon to cross Doctor's Gate, a Roman Road. Doctor's Gate is named after a Doctor Talbot, illegitimate son of the Earl of Shrewsbury, who was Vicar of Glossop from 1494 to 1550 because he used the route so frequently. A little further on Devil's Dike and a peat hag maze lead to Bleaklow. Here bogs, groughs and peaty channels make the Dark Peak live up to its name.

Where the Peak can be bleak, Toto's Coffee House and Bistro is always sunshine and smiles. In this bistro exotic fare like fresh calimari, Sardines, Jambalaya, BBQ's and home-made puddings go hand in hand with deep blue seas, azure, cloudless skies and heaven scented Mediterranean nights. It is the ideal venue for serenading senoritas and signoras.

**For further information, contact:**

**TOTO'S COFFEE HOUSE & BISTRO,
THE BASEMENT, 14 HIGH STREET EAST,
GLOSSOP, DERBYSHIRE,
SK13 8DA
TEL: 01457 865990**

# The Peppermill Restaurant
## Hayfield

The River Sett, which flows through Hayfield, is born in the Dark Peak where the Yoredale rocks and the millstone grit intermingle. It is a fascinating landscape that has about it an exhilarating savagery rather than picturesque.

There, at 622 metres (2,038ft), is Kinder Scout, the highest point in the Peak District. Like other Peak tops, Kinder is flat, a wedge of gritstone three miles long and one hundred feet thick. On its western edge, near the Downfall, huge horizontal slabs of grit dark grey in colour are exposed. The flat gritstone holds water so Kinder summit is mostly peat bog, a waste of brown fibrous mud cut up by cloughs, which are stream beds or deep ravines in shale. Unlike the limestone dales, the main valleys into which the cloughs flow are broad bottomed, green and habitable. Hayfield is in such a valley.

The Pennine Way starts from Edale on the south side of Kinder Scout and climbs Grindsbrook Clough to reach Kinder Plateau after two miles, which is crossed, westwards, to Crowdon Brook. The route then goes north over heather and peat, soon to follow the gentle River Kinder to Kinder Downfall, from where the scenery is spectacular.

The top of the Downfall marks the meeting of the Pennine Way's main and alternative routes. This mother of long distance walks then follows the rim of the plateau westwards, but by going left, southerly, still edging Kinder Plateau Red Brook is reached as it descends the boulders and gravel of the scarp. From here there is a path which descends to reach Hayfield in just over three miles.

Many fine walks radiate from Hayfield, including a pleasant one along a disused railway line down the valley bottom to New Mills.

However many people come to Hayfield to relax in the warm atmosphere of the family run Peppermill Restaurant. The surroundings are idyllic, overlooking Hayfield cricket ground, with views across the nearby hills. Choose a table on the balcony and listen to the murmur of the River Sett below or on a Saturday afternoon during summer watch a cricket match. You will be bowled over by the pleasant service and the high quality of The Peppermill Restaurant fare. The choice of course depends on what your appetite demands from afternoon cream teas and light snacks to a full à la carte menu. There is seating for up to eighty guests and family celebrations, like a wedding feast, are all part of the service.

Wholesome English food is the speciality, including a good vegetarian selection. On Wednesday, Thursday, Friday and Saturday evenings a value for money fixed price menu, including a starter, main course, dessert, coffee and mints, is very popular.

*Where to find us*

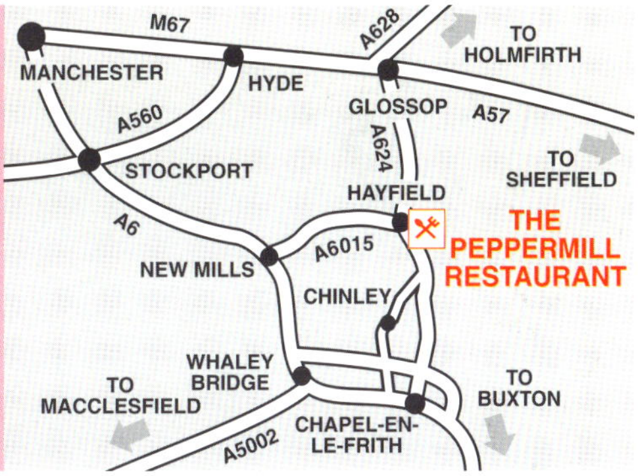


The Peppermill Restaurant is open all Sunday and on Wednesday to Saturday lunches, light snacks and afternoon teas are served from 12 noon to 3pm and evening meals from 7pm.

Be it Chicken Fettuccine or vegetarian Leek and Mushroom Crumble it is sure to be delicious.

**<u>For further information, contact:</u>**

**THE PEPPERMILL RESTAURANT,**
**17 CHURCH STREET,**
**HAYFIELD, STOCKPORT,**
**SK12 5JE**
**TEL: 01663 747812**

# Walk 1 - A Kind of Kinder

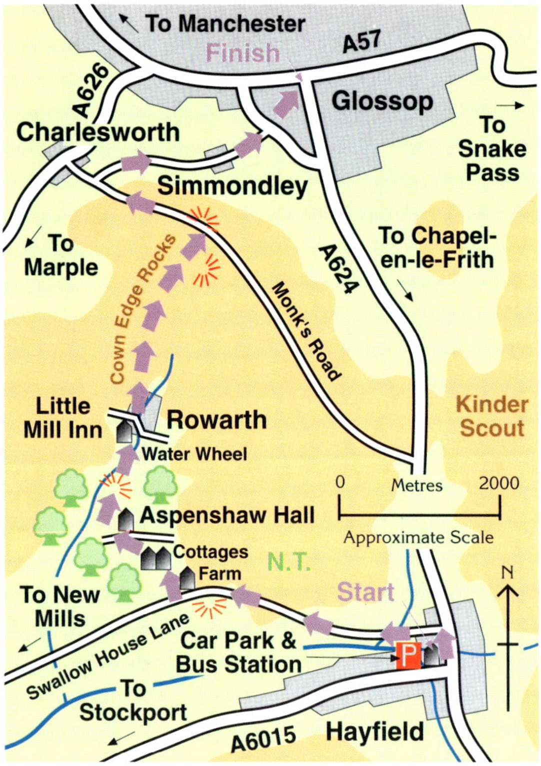


*Distance:* **5.75 Miles (9.2km)**

Hayfield has long been a mecca for ramblers since the 'Mass Trespass' on Kinder Scout in the 1920's. This walk offers a sample of the kind of walking country around Kinder.

Swallow House Lane, beyond Hayfield village, climbs steeply giving beautiful views over Hayfield. Walk over the brow of the hill, turning right at the signpost and entering a farmyard. Cross to a central gate and take the well-worn footpath by a wall. Drop down the hillside and cross the stile at the first old house surrounded by trees. Cross a large field to another stile. Turn left into the lane at the cottages to be suddenly surprised by the ivy-covered Aspenshaw Hall. The path enters woodland to the right, giving views over an unspoilt valley. Turn left into a lane beyond the farmyard and another surprise - a large water wheel splashes the stream. Turn into isolated Rowarth village to Cown Edge Rocks. A steep incline is negotiated to a long, straight track giving glimpses of the High Kinder Plateau over to the right. Turn left along Monk's Road and then right for Simmondley village. Keep going straight ahead for Glossop town centre. Buses back to Hayfield run hourly, up to 5.15pm.

# Walk 2 - Caverns' Circular

*Distance:* **3 Miles (4.8km)**

Around Castleton there is a great interior landscape of underground caverns. From the car park at Castleton take the riverside footpath to the heart of the village to follow a stream to a towering amphitheatre of limestone rocks at Peak Caverns. Return to the humpbacked bridge across the stream and climb Goosehill to the gravel path. This leads to open access National Trust land at the Longcliffe Estate. The path joins the lane at Speedwell Caverns, probably one of the most popular of the caverns due to it being flooded which allows for boat trips through its chambers.

Turn right at the cattle-grid to negotiate a steep climb to a stile in the side wall. The footpath then follows the contours of the valley to Treak Cliff Caverns. It is very steep here and the ground falls away swiftly to distant Hope Valley, so extra care is needed. Follow the path around the hillside to the famous Blue John Mines. Circling round, the path drops into Winnats Pass again by the stile.

Follow the side of the road through towering limestone rock faces. Return to Castleton either by the road, or retrace your steps across the Longcliffe Estate.

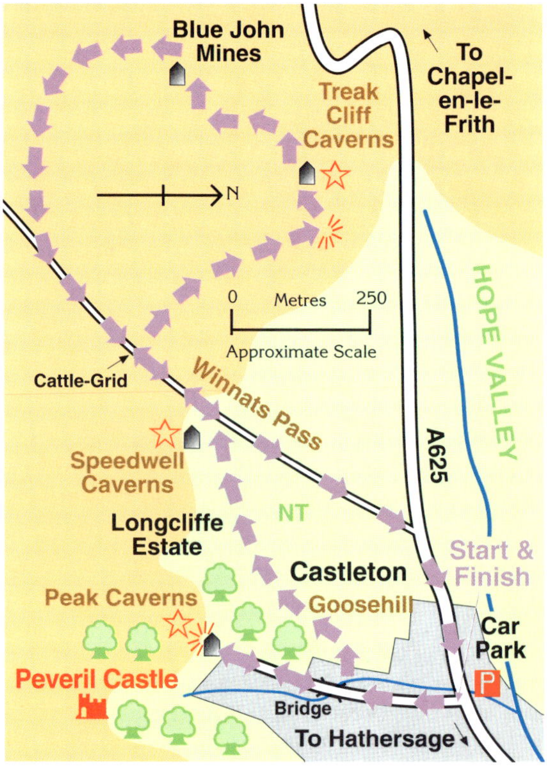

# Walk 3 - The Peaceful Dove

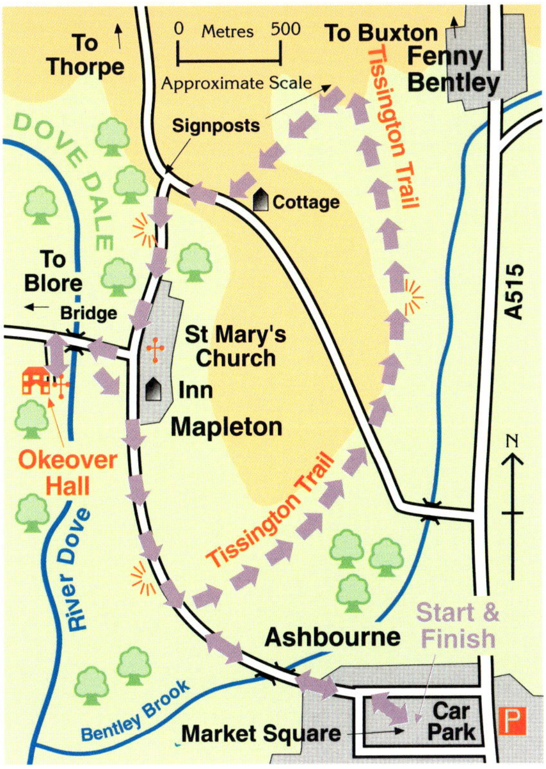


**Distance:** 3.75 Miles (6km)

Here is a beautiful countryside walk crossed by narrow lanes with old churches and ancient stately homes.

From the market square at the heart of the old market town of Ashbourne, follow the Tissington Trail signs to its entrance on Mapleton Road. The trail uses the bed of the former railway track which once crossed the Peak District from Buxton. Follow the trail for 1½ miles (2.4km) to a signpost for Fenny Bentley. Go left and take the stile out into the field. Climb the embankment to the stile at the top. Then cross over the large field to a cottage on the left. Turn right into the lane and left at the Mapleton signpost. The pleasant wooded valley of the Dove falls away to the right as the village of Mapleton is reached. Note lovely St Mary's Church which dates from 1750 and has an unusual dome shape. A humpbacked bridge crosses the lovely River Dove leading to stately Okeover Hall and another interesting old church with an ivy-encrusted tower. Return to the bridge and cross the field to the inn. Walk the peaceful river valley back to Ashbourne, or 'Esseburne', the 'brook of the ash tree' as it was known in the Domesday Book.

# Walk 4 - A Forest Foray

**Distance:** 3 Miles (4.8km)

On this foray into the heart of the forest of Macclesfield, start, by car, from the village of Langley and drive to the car park in the centre of the forest at Trentabank Reservoir.

From the car park walk eastwards down the lane, turning left into the Forest Trail. Turn right at the top to enter the village of Macclesfield Forest with its old chapel, famous for its rush bearing service in August of each year. Turn right at Charity Lane to the Information Centre at Standing Stone where views open out, extending across the whole of the Cheshire Plain towards the giant radio telescope of Jodrell Bank, said to be the greatest 'ear' on the universe in the world. The trail bears right through the forest and takes you back to the car park. On the eastern shore there is a nesting site of a large heronry, said to be the largest in the Peak District, the site beginning to be occupied early in March. The embankment at Ridgegate Reservoir, constructed in 1840, is a good place to observe the many facets of wildlife. Macclesfield Forest is a working forest and it is understood that all who visit the forest must comply with regulations for the well-being of all concerned.

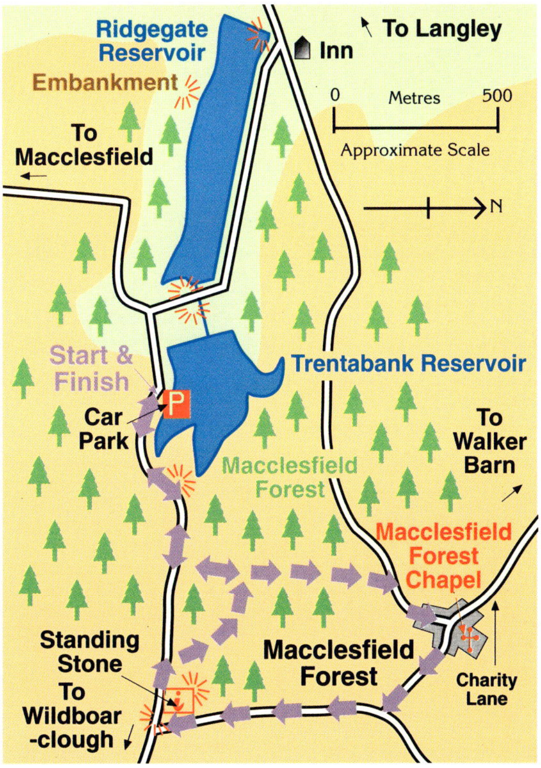

## Walk 5 - Village Tracks

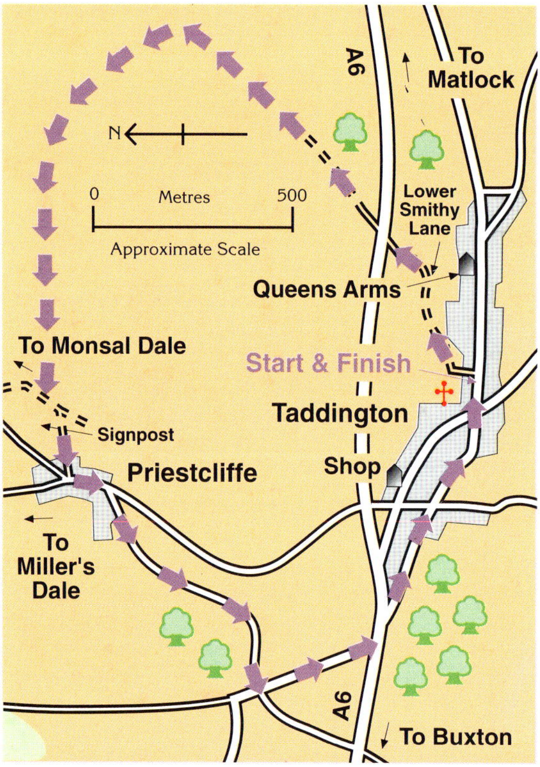


**Distance: 2.5 Miles (4km)**

Taddington is a large, long and narrow village with a shop and an inn. It is an isolated community close to the A6, Buxton to Matlock road. An unspoilt working village, it is less commercialised than most and very characteristic of the Peak District. From the main village street turn into the gravel lane called Lower Smithy Lane which meanders around numerous dry stone walls across the back regions of the village beyond the spired chapel until it enters the main road. Carefully cross the road and enter the track opposite.

The pleasant track circles between walls to an open valley, eventually coming to a gravel lane. Turn left, then first right, to enter the village of Priestcliffe. Take the higher lane back to the A6 where, on crossing to the pavement on the other side, a road leads back into Taddington. Near to Priestcliffe, a public footpath signpost points to Monsal Dale and Miller's Dale. If an extension to the walk is required the latter is less than a mile away. Monsal Dale is about three miles using part of the railway walkway. The original tunnels now on the walkway are closed to the public but provision is made by taking paths over them, finally leading to Monsal Dale.

## Walk 6 - Cathedral Walks

**Distance: 5 Miles (8km)**

Tideswell is one of the most attractive villages in the Peak District and its large, stone church is considered to be the 'Cathedral' of the Peak.

Go right at 'Poppies', past the church to the large square. Enter Sherwood Road and continue straight along the back of the town to open country. As the last building is passed and the road peters out to a track between low limestone walls, take the left hand turn and cross over this landscape of tiny limestone-walled enclosures towards leafy Miller's Dale. Join the main road turning right and then left for Litton Mill passing an old white-washed inn.

The lane follows the River Wye through a densely wooded gorge for some miles. Walk as much as you feel able and return to the main road by the inn. Before the great Rail Reform of 1965, Miller's Dale was once a major junction on the Midland Railway, running to St Pancras in London, a fact which is hard to believe now. It is now a walking track through to Monsal Dale. Return to Tideswell by the same track off the main road. Take the third left turn into a side lane which will add a variation on the return journey to town.

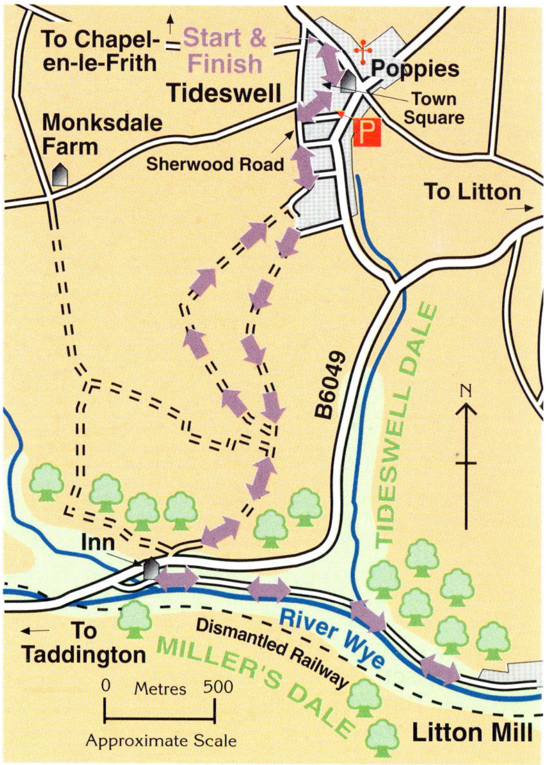

# Drive 1 - Across the High Plateau

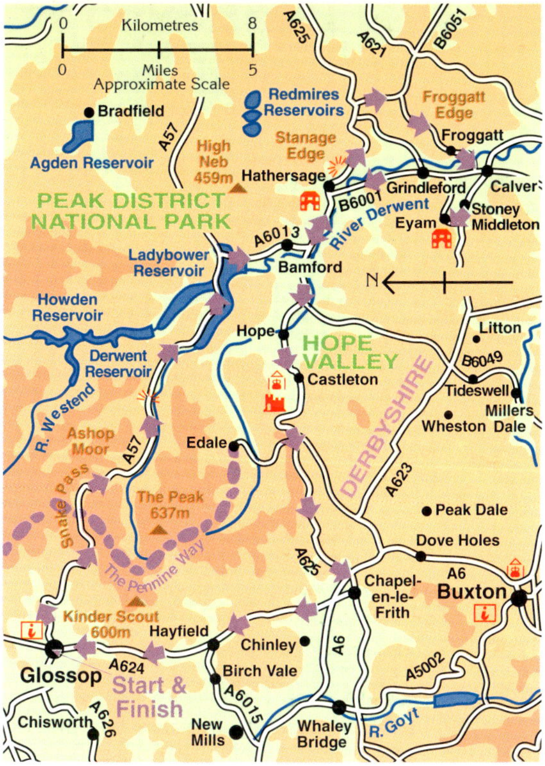


*Distance:* **50 Miles (80km)**

Between the two great cities of Manchester and Sheffield, in an area known as the Dark Peak, lies the mountain of Kinder Scout at 600 metres (2,000ft). From Glossop take the A57 Snake Pass road which opens out to this high Kinder plateau around the National Trust owned Ashop Moor. The road drops to the blue expanse of Ladybower Reservoir where the ruins of the lost village of Derwent may be seen when water levels are low.

Take the A6013, right, and turn left to Hathersage, well-known for its grave of the outlaw Little John. Here, the southern edge of the great rock escarpment of Stanage may be seen. At an acute bend, be careful to slow down to take the right turn for Chesterfield and then right again for Calver where there is an exciting rocky gorge known as Froggatt Edge. Head towards Chapel-en-le-Frith on the A623. Beyond the limestone rock faces of Stoney Middleton, turn right for the attractive village of Eyam. Turn left to Grindleford, and left again back to Hathersage on the B6001. Follow the A625 to Castleton and Chapel-en-le-Frith, flanking High Kinder again on the A624 passing Hayfield and returning to Glossop.

# Drive 2 - Where Peaceful Rivers Flow

*Distance:* **79 Miles (126.4km)**

This is a journey across the south-western region of the Peak. From Cheshire's hill country at Macclesfield, the way is to Rainow and Kettleshulme by the A5002 Whalley Bridge road. Here, a land of wooded valleys and rolling green hills is entered. Turn right at Kettleshulme for the Goyt Valley, passing Dunge Farm Gardens, a 2 hectare (5 acre) area of woodland, streams, ponds and landscaped gardens in a magnificent setting and open to the public. Drop by the Goyt Reservoir and take the one-way narrow track beyond the gorge to the main road.

Turn left and glide towards Buxton across a super moorland highway. Another good road, the A53, takes you to Leek, known as 'Queen of the Moorlands', passing the Roaches on the way, a strange rock formation and popular with climbers. Then onto the A523 to the market town of Ashbourne, noted for its Royal Shrove-Tide Football game. Return towards Buxton on the A515, turning left on the B5054 through Hartington, set in the rural heart of this Peak landscape. Turn right along the B5053, through Longnor and back to the A515. Go through Buxton to the A537 and return to Macclesfield.

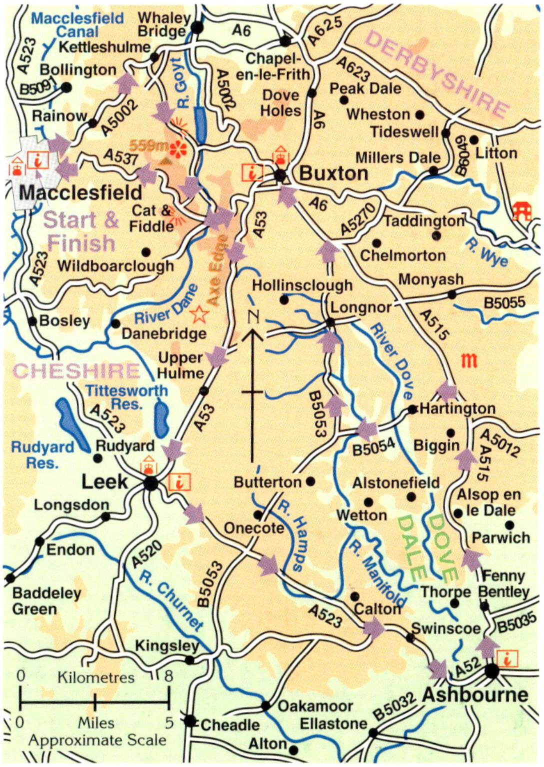

## Drive 3 - Pennine Wine

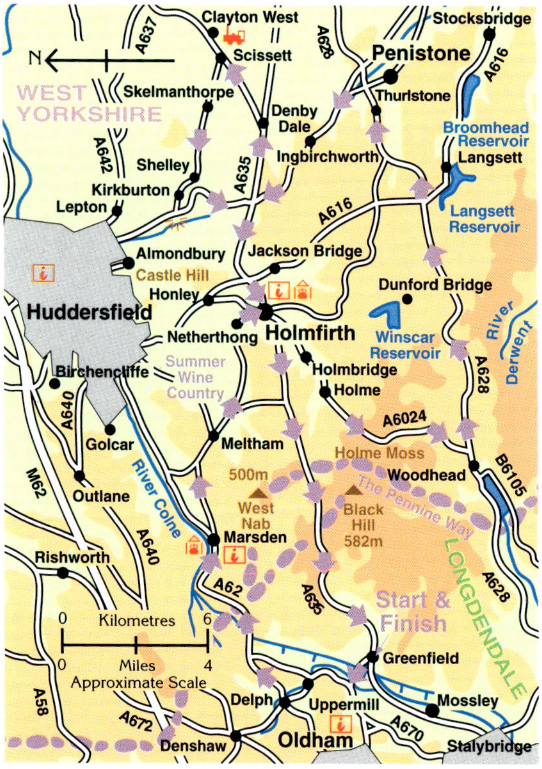


### *Distance:* 62 Miles (99.2km)

At Greenfield, near Oldham, the A670 speeds through Uppermill. Bear right towards Huddersfield onto the A62 into the Kirklees District, legendary resting place of the outlaw Robin Hood. At Marsden, turn right for the Pennine townships of Meltham and Netherthong. Continue to Holmfirth, well-known for the exploits of Compo and Co in the popular TV series. A large area of the Peak Park forms part of the 'Summer Wine' landscape and just outside Holmfirth, the 'millstone' symbol of the Peak Park is passed, under the shadow of the giant Holme Moss TV mast.

Take the A6024, one of the most exciting roads in the entire National Park, down to the reservoirs in Longdendale. Turn left along the A628 and at Penistone, follow the Huddersfield sign past the giant windmill farm to the road for Denby Dale. At Scissett, near the Kirklees Narrow Gauge Railway, turn left for Shelley and Kirkburton. As the Victoria Tower on Castle Hill comes into view, turn left at the junction and return to Holmfirth. Bear right on the A635 for Manchester. A straight open highway then crosses the Peak National Park, returning to Greenfield.

## Drive 4 - The Heart of the Park

### *Distance:* 69 Miles (110.4km)

This drive enters into the rural heart of the Peak District, starting at the award winning village of Tideswell. Turn right along the A623, going right again towards Wardlow and Monsal Dale. Enter the old village of Ashford, a beautiful waterside village so loved by many artists. Take the road for Baslow and follow the Chatsworth sign, passing through the great Chatsworth estate, the imposing home of the Duke and Duchess of Devonshire.

Join the A6 road beyond Beeley, turning left towards Darley Dale and Matlock. Continue on the A615 towards Alfreton and drive through Wessington, turning right for South Wingfield and Crich where there is a tramways' museum. At the A6, turn right into Cromford where Arkwright's factory first began the Industrial Revolution. Turn left to the village centre, then right for the A5012 to Buxton. Turn right along the B5056 and return to the A6 at Haddon Hall, a home with 800 years of history and open to the public. Turn left to Bakewell, and left again for Monyash. Here, turn right towards Flagg and Taddington, again re-joining the A6. Turn left and return to Tideswell using the minor road, right, through Miller's Dale.

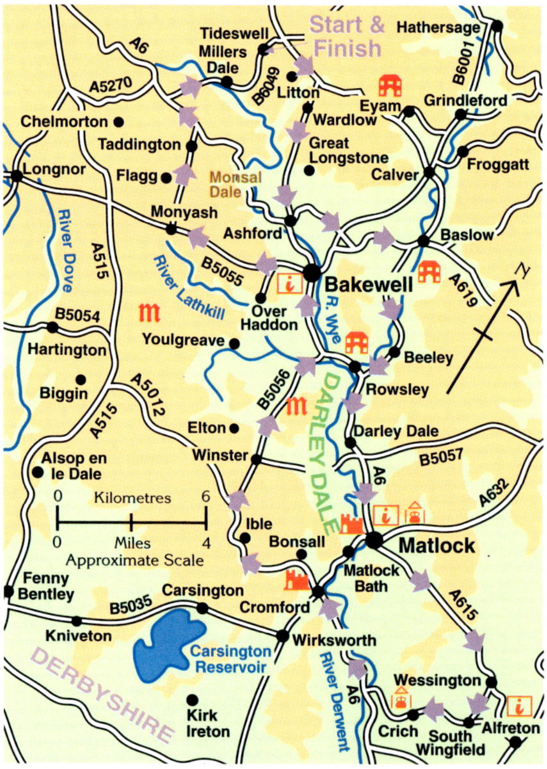

## Walk 7 - Plague Places

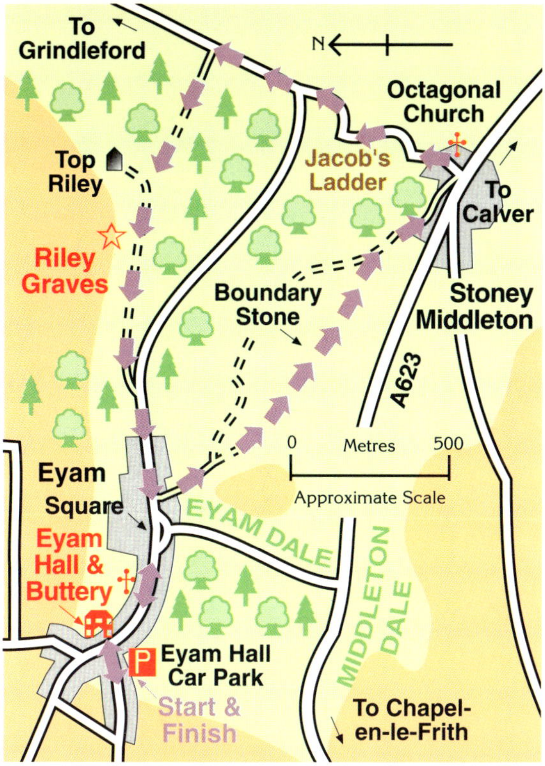


*Distance:* **3 Miles (4.8km)**

From Eyam Hall car park, turn right and walk to the square, passing Eyam Hall and the church on your left. Cross the square to the Lydgate, by the telephone kiosk and pillar box. Walk up the lane and at the top, continue straight on, along the footpath, through a 'squeeze' stile. Walk through several fields. Pass the Boundary Stone on your left and continue down the hill to the stile at the bottom.

Turn right and follow the track down into Stoney Middleton. Turn left and walk towards the octagonal church. Facing the church, take the lane to your left, up the hill, known as Jacob's Ladder. At the top, turn right along the road and after 300 metres go up the bridle path on the left.

Follow this path up through the wood. At the top of the hill you come out of the wood and join another path. Turn left along it, through woodland. Follow this path, visiting Riley Graves, in the field on your right, for a grim reminder of those distant days of the plague. Continue down the hill to the road. Turn right and, on reaching the square, retrace your steps to the car park, visiting Eyam Hall Buttery for refreshments en-route.

## Walk 8 - Viaduct Valley

*Distance:* **1.75 Miles (2.8km)**

The tall viaduct of the former railway which spans the River Wye at Monsal Dale is an interesting feature of this walk. From the car park at Upperdale continue to the crossroads at a group of cottages. Turn right to cross the River Wye. Here it widens almost to lake-size proportions, forming an attractive haven. The dirt track bends to climb towards the walkway of the former Midlands Railway track bed and crosses the viaduct high above Monsal Dale.

The railway line once crossed Derbyshire before its closure in 1968. The footpath then winds through woodlands and up the hillside to turn right for the road above where refreshments are available. This is also a lovely vantage point from where to look across the whole of Upper Dale and towards the wooded gorge of Monsal Dale. Continue down the track by the opposite bank and drop through the trees back into Upper Dale, marvelling at the construction of the huge viaduct now clearly visible through the trees on the left beyond the path. Follow the path to a small footbridge across the river and climb right taking the steep embankment back to the former bed of the rail track. Return to the car park at Upperdale.

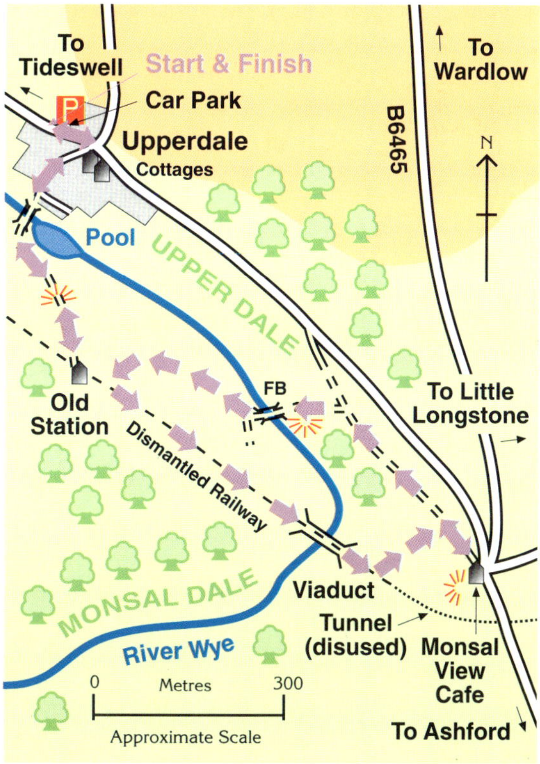

# Walk 9 - Heart of the Dairylands

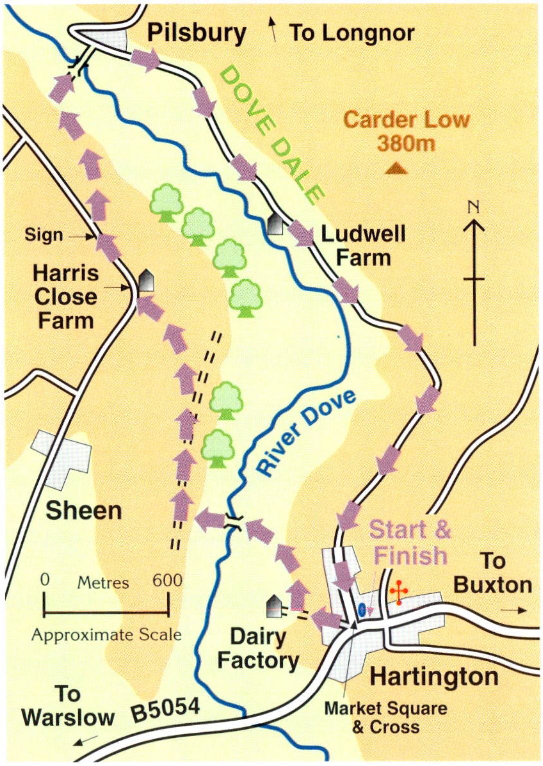


*Distance:* **4.5 Miles (7.2km)**

At the heart of the Peak District lies Hartington, an old world village surrounding a wide square with a broad village pond and an ancient market cross. Its old stone cottages provide a taste of old England in this beautiful corner of England. It is a large dairy centre and stands at the heart of a vast dairying and farming community, an area so characteristic of the Peak District.

From the square, take the lane out of the village to the large dairy factory and follow the meadow footpath through the various stiles to cross over the river Dove and climb to a rough lane. Turn right and then take the first footpath left across the hillside, eventually following the dry stone walling to the side of Harris Close Farm, a building dated 1842. Cross the farmyard, leaving it to enter the lane. Turn right along it.

At the signpost for Brund, take the footpath on the right and walk across the valley of the Dove to the village of Pilsbury, nestling under the shadow of Carder Low. From here, turn right into the narrow lane and follow it across the open moorlands through gates, returning to Hartington.

# Walk 10 - The Heights of Abraham

*Distance:* **4 Miles (6.4km)**

This walk may be taken in two parts with entrance to Riber Castle and Country Park being optional. From the car park by the side of the river Derwent, opposite the inn, turn left for Matlock Bath. Cross the bridge and go under the railway arch. A large poster says, 'Welcome to the Heights of Abraham'. A cable car crosses the rocky gorge to a 60 acre Country Park high above the town where a Country Trail may be followed. From the gate of the park follow the woodland footpath steeply down to Matlock Bath which enters Orchard Road. Take steps down to a passage, turning left at the promenade, into an area very much resembling a Cornish fishing port. Coming down, views extend up to Riber Castle, our next destination.

From the railway station turn left, back to the 'Heights' poster at the arch via the woodland lane by the river. A stile on the right leads to Starkholmes village. Turn right to climb Riber Road. By a cottage, turn left to climb the footpath to Riber Castle, which is now a wildlife park. From Riber Hall, wind down the lane and turn left. At an inn a footpath opposite leads back to Matlock Bath and the A6. Retrace your steps to the car park.

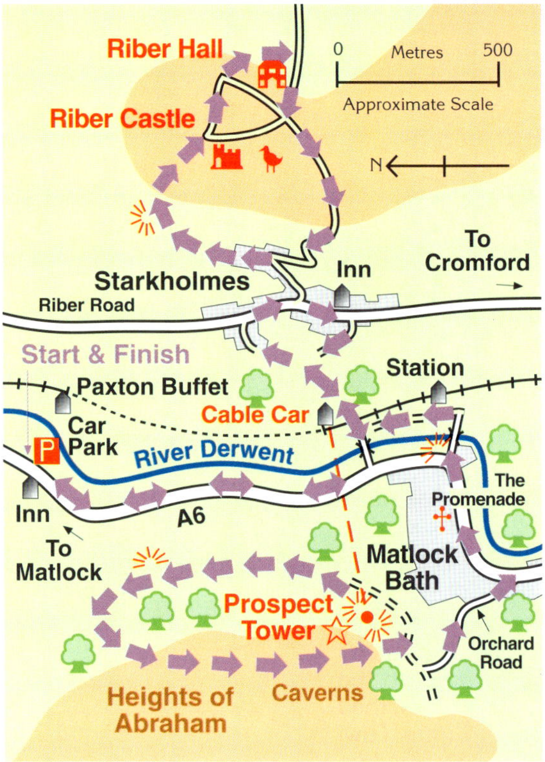

# Walk 11 - Vintage Views

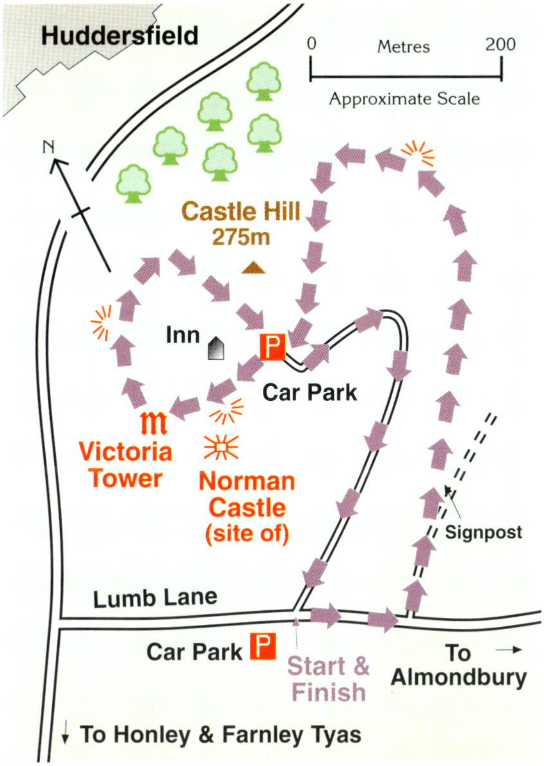


**Distance: 1 Mile (1.6km)**

Just north, between the villages of Honley and the dark gritstone hilltop village of Farnley Tyas and close to the woodland township of Almondbury is the huge prehistoric earthwork known as Castle Hill which takes its name from the castle built early in the C12th by the De Laci family. This surprisingly easy-going walk provides superb panoramic views across the town of Huddersfield, surrounding Summer Wine Countryside and the Peak National Park.

Start from the car park at the base of the earthwork and walk down Lumb Lane to a gravel footpath. Turn left at the next footpath sign. Come to a stile and bear right taking the central path that climbs slightly away from the stile. Follow the footpath round, eventually arriving at a path of stone slabs. Follow these to a large open expanse of grassy sward at the top of Castle Hill, 275 metres (900ft), where the strange looking Victoria Tower is found. It is open, in summer, on Bank Holidays and weekend afternoons. The tower is 30.17 metres (100ft) high with 165 steps and was built in 1897 to commemorate the 60th anniversary of Queen Victoria's reign. The little road leads back down to the car park at the foot of the mound.

# Walk 12 - A Buxton Town Trail

**Distance: 2 Miles (3.2km)**

After morning coffee and biscuits, sample this short trail through the town at a leisurely pace, to be back at Miller's restaurant in time for a delicious meal.

From Spring Gardens, turn right, circling round towards the Crescent which was modelled on the town of Bath, with its natural spring baths, once used by Roman soldiers. Pass the Old Hall Hotel, once visited by Mary Queen of Scots. Turn right into the square and pass the jewel in Buxton's crown - The Buxton Opera House. Opposite is a Victorian letterbox which is unique in Derbyshire. Pass St John's Church, built in Italian Tuscan style, and the Devonshire Royal Hospital, with its unsupported dome of 47 metres (154ft), built in 1880 and said to be the largest of its kind in the world. St John's Road leads to the Pavilion Gardens with its Concert Hall and onto the picturesque walkway, 'The Broadwalk'. Turn right onto Bath Road. At St Ann's Well, sample Buxton's spa water, believed to have powers to cure the sick. Turn left along High Street to the Market Place with its C15th market cross, the highest market in England. Go between the Town Hall and museum, passing The Slopes and returning to the start.

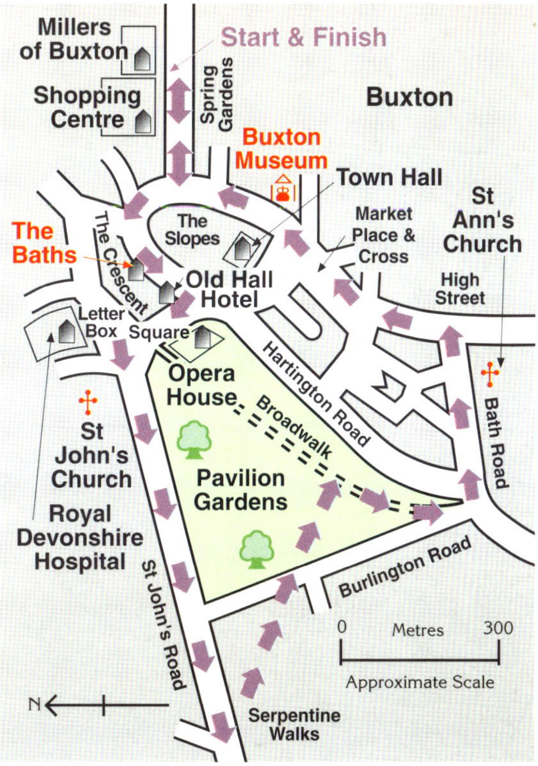

# The Paxton Buffet
## Matlock

Once a waiting room at Matlock Railway Station, terminus of the branch line from Derby, Paxton Buffet is far from the one depicted in 'Brief Encounter'.

There it was all steamy tea urns, hot Bovril, rock-hard rock buns and railway sandwiches curling at the edges! Here the contrast could hardly be greater, thanks to proprietor Shirley Hitchcock's concern for your creature comforts.

While relaxing in a cosy atmosphere awash with memorabilia of yesteryear, she and her happy helpers will set you at ease with friendly chat and a crackling open fire will endorse that warmth as you ponder on which of her home-made creations will suit you best.

The cheese and onion pie is tempting with perhaps apple pie and fresh cream to follow. How about some mushy peas, toasties or maybe some pasties? The jacket potatoes are tasty and filling, but so is the bread pudding. Fancy some scones with butter and jam, home-made mincemeat and marmalade with, to wash it down, some tea, coffee, chocolate or a cold drink? All and more is available.

There is seating inside and out and there are facilities for changing your baby if needed.

The Paxton Buffet is open seven days a week, usually between 9.30am and 5pm in winter and later during the rest of the year.

That section of the Midland main line running from St Pancras to Manchester through the limestone country of the Peak was opened as far as Rowsley in 1849 and reached Manchester by 1867.

It cut through some of the most spectacular scenery in the Peak and this created magnificent examples of Victorian railway construction in England. Between Matlock and twenty miles distant Buxton ten tunnels and many viaducts and bridges were built, the largest being the 30.5 metres (100ft) high, five arched structure at Monsal Dale. Passenger services north of Matlock were withdrawn in 1967, the line closed in 1968 and most of the track was removed.

The Peak Planning Board acquired the track inside the National Park and during the 1970s the Monsal Trail was created over part of it.

In 1975 the Peak Railway Society, forerunner of today's Peak Rail PLC, was formed with the aim of re-opening all the line between Matlock and Buxton. After many years of hard work, during which a temporary platform, Matlock Riverside, was built, the two miles of track between there and Darley Dale was formally inaugurated by the Duke of Devonshire in May, 1992.

It is hoped that in the not too distant future Peak Rail will be running into the main station alongside The Paxton Buffet where future passengers can sample Shirley's fine fare.

Other local attractions like Riber Castle, the cable cars at Matlock Bath, Chatsworth House and the puddings at Bakewell can wait until you have sampled Shirley's home-baking. For like Peak Rail, The Paxton Buffet is on the right track.

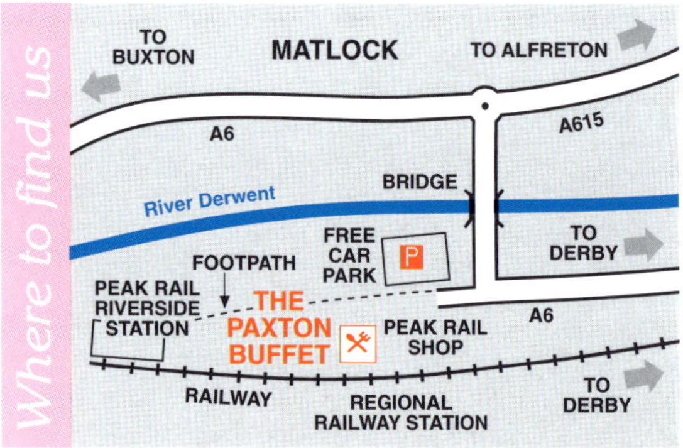


**For further information, contact:**

**THE PAXTON BUFFET,
MATLOCK RAILWAY STATION,
MATLOCK, DERBYSHIRE,
DE4 3NA
TEL: 01629 580381**

# Beresford Arms Hotel
## Ashbourne

Ashbourne, the gateway to the Peak, is a pretty town of cobbled streets and delightful shops, a swimming pool and leisure facilities. It sits comfortably on the border of the Peak District National Park, ringed by hills, some of which rise to 183 metres (600ft).

It is at Ashbourne that the famous Shrove Tide 'football' match is played annually. It is a free for all game played on a pitch that is three miles long. The game was played in the Middle Ages and is between the Up'ards, those who live to the north of Henmore Brook, which runs through the middle of the town, and the Down'ards, who live south of the Stream. The goals were once marked by mill wheels but today the Up'ards goal is the spindle of the old wheel and the Down'ards goal is a stone plaque. There are two separate matches, one on Shrove Tuesday and one on Ash Wednesday and each game can last up to eight hours, from 2pm until 10pm.

There is an abundance of old almshouses in Ashbourne, the oldest being the Owfield Almshouses in Church Street. They date from 1640 but the upper storeys were added in 1848. Pegge's Almshouses, single storey dwellings built about 1669 of local sandstone and now private homes, stand next to the Owfield Almshouses. Near to them are some more, clergy Widows' Almshouses. These were built in 1753 for the widows of Anglican clergy. Others, Spaldens Almshouses, were built in 1723 near St Oswald's churchyard.

St Oswald's is noted for its many ornamental tombs, the most impressive being those of two local families the Cockaynes and the Boothbys. During the Civil War three cannon balls are said to have been fired at the church by parliamentary troops. The dents they made can still be seen in the west wall. St Oswald's Church dates from 1241 and its lectern and pulpit are decorated with Blue John from Castleton. The churchyard gateposts have an unusual design of obelisks standing on skulls and flames.

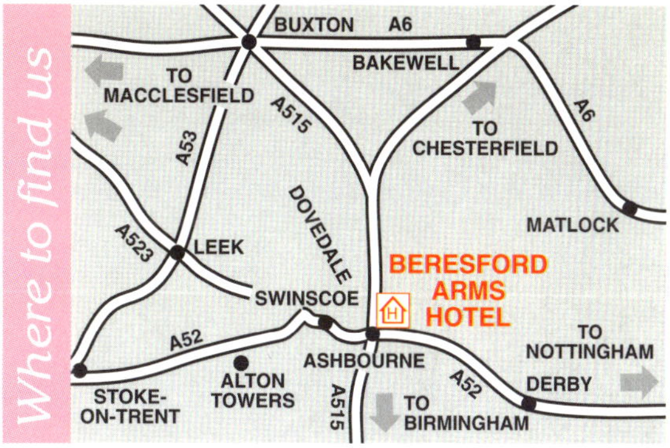


Beresford Arms Hotel stands opposite the old Ashbourne railway station, and was built at the turn of the century. It has a peaceful modern Lounge Bar offering a wide selection of real ales, beers, wines, spirits, including malt whiskies, and minerals, along with an excellent bar food menu, tea and coffee. All are available throughout the day.

The restaurant, with its à la carte and bar menu, is particularly attractive and the excellent fare includes home-made pies and hot pots. The Beresford Specialty Sunday Luncheon is a great favourite with the discerning guest.

The accommodation is furnished to a high standard with all bedrooms having en-suite facilities, colour TV, tea and coffee making facilities, direct-dial telephone and trouser press. There is ample car parking.

Breakfast is from 7.30am to 10am with bar meals from 11am to 11pm.

Children and pets are made most welcome and special weekend and short stay breaks are available.

**For further information, contact:**

**BERESFORD ARMS HOTEL,<br>STATION ROAD, ASHBOURNE,<br>DERBYSHIRE, DE6 1AA<br>TEL: 01335 300035<br>FAX: 01335 300065**

# The Dog & Partridge Country Inn

## Swinscoe

For a culture vulture with a penchant for literature seeking a secluded haven far from the madding crowd and set in a countryside walkers and sightseers refer to as paradise, the hamlet of Swinscoe is the very spot. For there at The Dog and Partridge, a C17th country inn and motel with olde worlde bar and thirty en-suite rooms, the proprietor, Mrs Mary Stelfox, and her friendly staff will cosset you while you indulge in your desires.

Ashbourne, about four miles east of Swinscoe, was visited regularly by the C19th novelist George Eliot, whose real name was Mary Ann Evans. She described the place as a 'pretty town within sight of the blue hills'. In her novel 'Adam Bede', Ashbourne is Oakbourne and the surrounding district, with its 'wide-scattered grey stone houses' is Stonyshire. She called the 65 metres (212ft) high tapering spire of St Oswald's Church the finest single spire in England.

George Eliot was not the only writer fond of Ashbourne. Izaak Walton frequently fished in the area and the town hall is on the site of the Talbot Inn, in which he set some of 'The Compleat Angler'.

Dr Samuel Johnson, the writer and lexicographer often stayed with his friend Dr John Taylor in a C17th building, The Mansion, in Church Street. It is now a boarding school for girls.

Among the famous but not literary people associated with Ashbourne is Catherine Booth co-founder of the Salvation Army, who was born there in 1829.

In 1745 when Bonnie Prince Charlie was retreating from Derby to Scotland, he stayed one night in Ashbourne Hall, then the seat of the Cockayne family.

Swinscoe is situated on the Derbyshire - Staffordshire border on the fringe of that beautiful part of the White Peak through which the picturesque River Manifold flows to its confluence with the equally lovely River Dove.

It is an area renowned for the high quality of its walks and attracts hikers like honey attracts bears.

Traditional ales are available in the well stocked bar of The Dog and Partridge as are other ales, lagers, cider and stout, wines and spirits, including a wide range of malts.

The restaurant seats eighty, has a table d'hote menu and is open every day from 11am until 11pm. Sunday luncheon is served there from 12noon until 4.30pm.

Breakfast is served between 7.30am and 10am and morning coffee, bar meals, afternoon teas from 11am to 11pm daily. There is also an à la carte menu.

Staffordshire Oatcakes are very popular at The Dog and Partridge; and their fillings include Chicken and Mushroom, Sea Food, Stilton or Leek and Apple.

For families with young children there are indoor and outdoor play areas with their Fisher Price toys.

Should the urge for more excitement come to the fore, the famous Alton Towers, with its thrills and mind blowing rides, is only a few miles away.

So there it is, all you could wish for at The Dog and Partridge Country Inn.

*Where to find us*

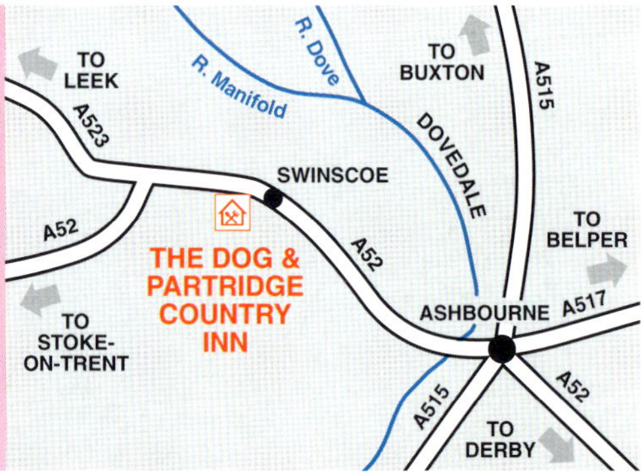


**For further information, contact:**

**THE DOG & PARTRIDGE COUNTRY INN,**
**SWINSCOE, ASHBOURNE,**
**DERBYSHIRE, DE6 2HS**
**TEL: 01335 343183**
**FAX: 01335 342742**

# The Charles Cotton Hotel

## Hartington

Hartington, 'Stag's' hill, was first recorded in the Domesday Book as 'Harteoum'. It lies above the 200 metres (700ft) contour in the gentle Dove Valley. During the Middle Ages it was an important market centre with a large and elaborate stone church. Today it is a picturesque village with a pond and a cluster of gift shops and tea rooms. It is famed for its cheese factory.

Recently, during a local doctor's investigation into a condition called goitre or 'Derbyshire Neck', which is common in the neighbourhood, he found that ninety percent of the people living there had been born there. This is an uncommon statistic that speaks highly of Hartington's appeal.

The typical limestone scenery of the White Peak is a gently sloping plateau slit with gorges so abrupt and narrow that they are often not seen until you are almost on top of them. It is these gorges or dales that inspired Ruskin to comment 'The whole glory of the country is in its dales'. Each has its charm, its individuality; but many acclaim Dovedale to outweigh the rest.

It was in this most agreeable dale that Izaak Walton, author of 'The Compleat Angler', and his great friend poet and fellow fisherman Charles Cotton, spent much of their lives happily contemplating the River Dove, which Izaak Walton called 'The finest river that I have ever seen and the fullest of fish'.

Charles Cotton was born at Beresford Hall, near Hartington in the C17th and resided in the village. He introduced Izaak Walton to the Peak and was in fact joint author of 'The Compleat Angler'.

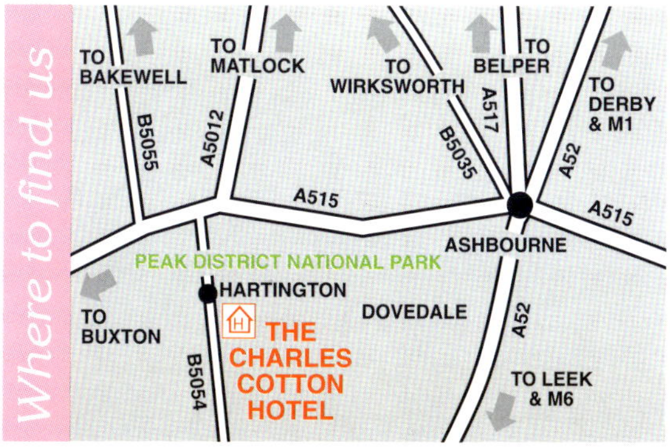


This stone-built, C15th hotel, which is named after Hartington's most famous son, has sixteen rooms, a comfortable lounge bar, restaurant, tea room and beer garden with a children's play area.

The hotel has a reputation for excellent hospitality and home-cooking. Breakfasts and traditional Sunday lunch are served in the main hotel where the restaurant has an à la carte menu. Morning coffee and afternoon tea are served in the tea room. Bar meals are served in both.

A popular speciality is Staffordshire oatcakes with various fillings like mushrooms, chicken and mushroom, Stilton, leek and apple and sea food.

Breakfasts are served from 7.30am until 10am, lunches are available all day and the tea room is open from 9am until 6pm.

The hotel has a selection of accommodation from en-suite rooms to family rooms and ground floor bedrooms suitable for the disabled.

Children are catered for and there is a baby listening facility in all rooms, along with high chairs and cots, and pets are welcome.

On winter days you can relax in their friendly bar, cheered by a roaring log fire. A fine malt makes an excellent adjunct to a blazing hearth and the hotel has a wide selection of fine whiskies. If longer drinks are to your taste, there are traditional ales, ciders, lagers, stout and wines.

**For further information, contact:**

**THE CHARLES COTTON HOTEL,**
**HARTINGTON, BUXTON,**
**DERBYSHIRE,**
**SK17 OAL**
**TEL: 01298 84229**

# Queens Arms

## Taddington

It was the Anglo Saxons who first settled at the 'tun' of Tata's people in the C5th, creating a settlement now known as Taddington. The Roman army had withdrawn to Gaul and the Saxons from north Germany and the Angles from south Denmark saw their chance, for in Roman Britannia, hitherto inhabited by Celts, not only loot and gold awaited, but land. They came in droves, bringing their families with them, and despite being held back by two Roman-British commanders, Ambrosius Aurelianus and legendary Arthur, were gradually absorbed into the land. They intermarried, built settlements and raised crops on cultivation terraces or strip lynchets, one of which remains at Taddington. So Britannia became the land of the Angles and Saxons, England; and Taddington is proud of its part in that transformation.

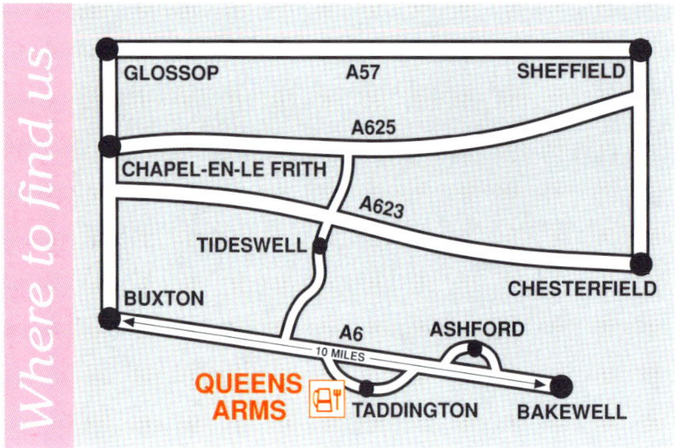


This linear, working village at 335 metres (1100ft) one of the highest in Derbyshire, owes its location to its original water supply. A unique feature is the pattern of 'water lanes' that lead from the main road to the 'High Well'.

In 1820 Robert Blincoe published 'Some Passages of the Life of a London Parish Prentice at Litton and Cressbrook Mills' in which he exposed the harshness of factory life for child labour. The unmarked graves of twenty of these children, who died while in apprenticeship, are in Taddington churchyard. The two nearby mills are now ruinous.

Between Taddington and four miles distant Ashford lies Taddington Dale, designated as a site of special scientific interest because of its ancient ash and wych-elms and rare limestone loving plants. There are seventeen miles of footpaths in the parish, along which one hundred and twenty species of wild flowers grow.

One of the fonts in Taddington church was once used for washing beer tankards in The Star Inn. There were once four pubs in the village and every Whit Tuesday Taddington's Oddfellows had a ball when a Morris Dance, the rigmarole 'Puddin in a Lantern' was sung and danced outside all of them.

The Queens Arms is Taddington's only remaining pub with a unique character because everything that is purveyed by mine hosts, Peter and Maria, is free from nonsense and affectation: all is real: real ale, real home-cooked food, served beside a real fire. As one local put it: 'They know their business and when you see the trouble they take with their ale and food you know they will take good care of customers. That is why the place has a warm friendly atmosphere where regulars feel at home and strangers are made welcome and can join in the locals' conversation'.

From June until October the pub is open all day. Otherwise Monday to Saturday 10am to 3pm and 7pm to 11pm and Sunday from 12 noon until 3pm and 7pm to 10.30pm.

In living memory the cellar was used as the village mortuary. As the coachmen on the Sheffield to Manchester Turnpike road used to say 'There's non buried in the churchyard who lived in the parish and only those who were deaf, dumb and blind were in the churchyard'. Call in at the Queens Arms and find out for yourself.

**For further information, contact:**

**QUEENS ARMS,**
**MAIN ROAD, TADDINGTON,**
**BUXTON, DERBYSHIRE,**
**SK17 9UD**
**TEL: 01298 85245**

# The Lamb Inn
## Hayfield Road, Chinley

Cheshire is shaped like a teapot with industrial Lancashire on its lid and its base resting on rural Shropshire. There are hills on either side. Westward lie the Welsh mountains and the Derbyshire Pennines are to the east. There, in Chinley is a real treasure of a pub, The Lamb Inn.

To many people during the 30s, 40s and 50s Chinley was noted for its huge marshalling yard, which contained the only turntable for trains in the Manchester area.

Nowadays Chinley has become a base from which to explore the surrounding countryside and with good reason. For nearby are South Head Mountain leading to Edale, Cracken Edge leading to Hayfield, Eccles Pike with its wonderful views, Coombes Reservoir with its fishing, Chapel-en-le-Frith with its golf club and, a fifteen minute drive away at Castleton, the Peak, Speedwell, Treak Cliff and Blue John Caverns.

Many discerning people come to Chinley, some to tackle the wonderful, local walks, others simply to enjoy a jolly good meal in a relaxed atmosphere. Many, having discovered The Lamb Inn, return regularly either for morning coffee, a snack or an extensive bar meal, lunch, dinner or traditional Sunday lunch.

The Lamb Inn was originally built as three cottages for quarry workers in 1759. The road alongside which they were built became obsolete when a by-pass was built and this redundant road now serves as a large car park for about fifty vehicles.

Susan and Noel Burrows own and run this excellent establishment. Noel, thirty years in the pub trade, trained as chef at a catering college in Manchester, the Dorchester, London and the Midland Hotel, Manchester. But he is best known as an internationally famous crown green and flat green bowler.

The most popular item on the menu of more than thirty main meals, including Fisherman's Crumble, Mixed Grill, Scampi and Lasagne, is home-made Steak and Kidney Pie. Then there are the daily specials and the delicious vegetarian dishes.

Two of The Lamb Inn's five quaint rooms have coal fires. The pub also has a pleasant patio cum outside eating area. It is residential (bed and breakfast), with two en-suite double rooms and one en-suite twin room, all with TV.

Should you fancy a drink in the bar, you will be spoilt for choice. There are Stones, Carling, McEwans Export, Becks, Guinness, Tennants' Extra and L.A. Marston's Pedigree, Bass Dark Mild, Strongbow Cider, wines by the glass and all popular spirits.

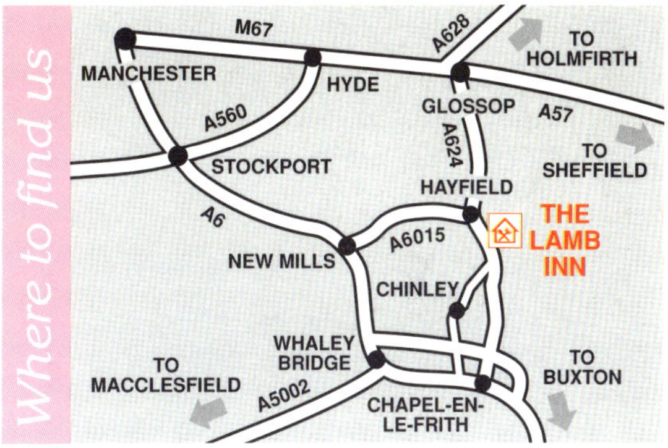


Throughout the year The Lamb Inn is open Monday to Friday for lunches until 2.30pm and for evening meals from 6pm until 10.30pm. On Saturdays and Sundays it is open all day for food until 10.30pm. Between April 1st and October 31st sandwiches are available until 6pm, but not between November 1st and March 31st.

**For further information, contact:**

**THE LAMB INN,**
**HAYFIELD ROAD,**
**CHINLEY, STOCKPORT,**
**CHESHIRE, SK12 6AL**
**TEL: 01663 750519**

# Monsal View Cafe

## Monsal Head, Bakewell

During the 1860s the site the cafe now occupies was the pay office and sleeping quarters for the railway labourers who were building the line from London to Manchester, its most spectacular construction being the famous five arched viaduct over the River Wye. The line, opened in 1863, cut through the heart of England's 'Little Switzerland' and was spoken of with admiration by successive generations of railway enthusiasts. Yet its construction was bitterly opposed by many who saw it as being detrimental to the dale.

In 1867 Ruskin eloquently expressed these feelings when writing about the viaduct. 'There was a rocky valley between Buxton and Bakewell, once upon a time divine as the Vale of Tempe: you might have seen the Gods there morning and evening, Apollo and all the sweet Muses of the light walking in fair procession on the lawns of it, and to and fro among the pinnacles of its crags. You cared neither for Gods nor grass but for cash (which you did not know the way to get): you thought you could get it by what The Times calls 'Railroad Enterprise'. You enterprised a railroad through the valley, you blasted its rocks away, heaped thousands of tons of shale into its lovely streams. The valley is gone and the Gods with it and now every fool in Buxton can be at Bakewell in half an hour, and every fool in Bakewell at Buxton: which you think a lucrative process of exchange you fools everywhere.'

For passengers travelling from St Pancras to Manchester it was the spectacular way and when the swaying expresses thundered through a tunnel straight onto Monsal viaduct it was a tremendous thrill. When, in 1968, the line was closed the opposition to the demolition of Monsal viaduct was so overwhelming that the structure was left standing and remains part of the landscape.

During the line's life the Monsal View Cafe was a station master's residence. From there refreshments were sold to hikers, tourists and motorists, just as the cafe does today in a more upmarket way.

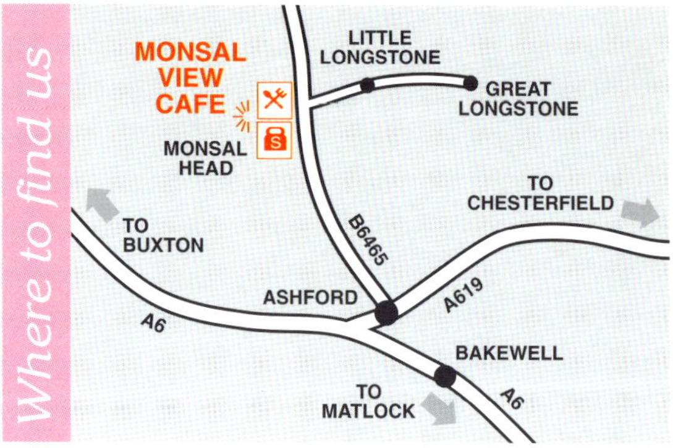


Here are some forty covers, farmhouse tables, tea chests, and a roaring log fire in winter. There is a room displaying a scatter of old tins and advertisements which recall a slice of yesteryear. Visitors partake of morning coffee, cream teas, afternoon teas and lunches in a relaxed atmosphere.

The soup is excellent, as is the Yorkshire Pudding filled with beef stew. Salads and curries are available and sandwiches are made to order. And, yes the cakes really are all home-made. There is a table licence and the beer, lager, spirits and wine make a fine accompaniment to all the good food.

Mugs of tea, coffee, sandwiches, sweets and ice cream are sold in the garden snack bar, which overlooks Monsal Dale.

Between the end of March and the end of October the cafe is open 10.30am to 5pm seven days a week. It is closed on Thursdays during November, February and March. In December it is closed Monday to Friday, except the Christmas Holiday, and during the last three weeks of January it is closed. So to avoid being disappointed please check the opening times carefully. It is too good to miss.

**For further information, contact:**

**MONSAL VIEW CAFE,**
**MONSAL HEAD,**
**BAKEWELL, DERBYSHIRE,**
**DE45 1NL**
**TEL: 01629 640346**

# Armitage's Garden Centres

## Shelley & Birchencliffe, Huddersfield

In 1842 William Armitage welcomed his first customer to his small, well stocked corn and seed warehouse in New Street, Huddersfield. Since then the people of West Yorkshire have turned to Armitage's for practically everything to do with gardening. In that year William's son joined him and since then the family name has remained, maintaining the traditional values on which the company was established.

Moves and expansions have taken place regularly and today Armitage's Garden Centres offer the widest possible choice of merchandise all the year round to gardeners and garden lovers from their Pennine Garden Centre at Shelley, sited at the gateway to Summer Wine Country, and Mower World and Garden Centre at Birchencliffe.

The Armitage family is proud to invite the discerning gardener to enjoy the relaxing atmosphere of the long established and traditional Pennine Garden Centre in the heart of Kirklees countryside at Shelley. It is the first step along the path to gardening success because it boasts one of the largest and most varied selections of plants, trees and shrubs in West Yorkshire, specifically selected for the suitability of the local climate. Every one is carefully displayed, labelled with a colour illustration and planting instructions.

From springtime, when a gardener's fancy turns to thoughts of a beautiful garden, through the glorious days of summer, the time to really enjoy your garden, to the golden days of autumn, Armitage's staff are fully qualified to give expert advice in any area of gardening. Flower and vegetable seeds, gardening accessories, greenhouses, sheds, fencing, ornaments, barbecues, pools and fish, bulbs and house plants in rich variety are all available at both centres.

In addition to its garden centre, Mower World at Birchencliffe has probably the most complete choice of garden machinery you have ever seen. There are mowers of all types for every size of garden, scarifiers, hedge trimmers, electrical and mechanical saws, weeders and cultivators. Be it 'stand up and push' or 'sit on and ride', Armitage's have got it and can advise you.

A wide range of machines is available for hire and a comprehensive warranty and back up service are provided on all items. Similarly the service department can recondition and repair your old garden equipment at extremely competitive rates. Armitage's have literally thousands of spare parts for most makes of mowers in stock and available seven days a week in season.

Both of Armitage's Garden Centres have warm, airy and cheerful coffee shops where you can enjoy anything from a cup of tea or coffee to a snack or light lunch in pleasant surroundings. The one at Shelley has particularly aesthetic views of the local countryside. The popular refreshment areas offer a pleasant break from your shopping and blend so effectively into the background.

Armitage's Garden Centres are a growing success, their aim to offer a service unrivalled throughout the North of England is blossoming and it is the customer who enjoys the taste of the fruit.

*Where to find us*

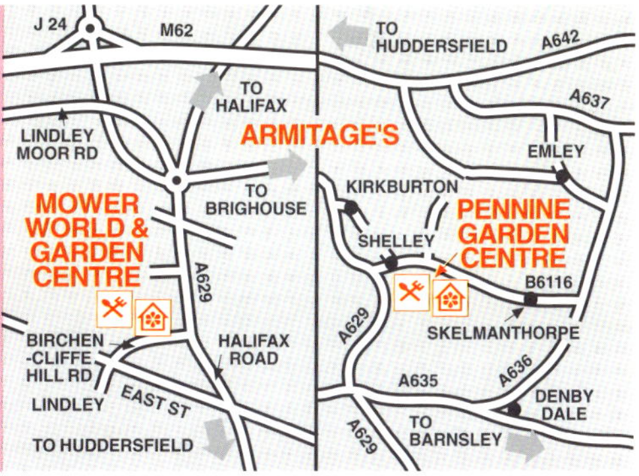


**For further information, contact:**

**ARMITAGE'S GARDEN CENTRES,**
**HUDDERSFIELD ROAD, SHELLEY,**
**HUDDERSFIELD, W YORKS, HD8 8LG**
**TEL SHELLEY: 01484 607248**
**OR BIRCHENCLIFFE: 01484 536010**

# Setter Dog Inn

## Walker Barn, Macclesfield

The south western edge of the Peak District is an area of open, sometimes treeless, moorland drained by three river systems: the Churnet, the Dane and the Goyt. One of its most interesting towns is Macclesfield, famed for its textiles. It houses a Silk Mill and Heritage Centre which is the only museum in Britain devoted to the silk industry.

Nearby is the Paradise Silk Mill where guides demonstrate weaving. They work the twenty-six hand-powered Jacquard looms in their original setting, restored to demonstrate the skills of a dying art.

Tegg's Nose Country Park lies east of Macclesfield. It is based around an old sandstone quarry; and various fine walks begin at its car park. The Gritstone Trail, a 20 mile path from Lyme Park to Ruston, near Leek, which links with The Staffordshire Way, passes through Tegg's Nose Country Park.

Another famous walk, The Middlewood Way, links Macclesfield with 11 miles distant Middlewood. Cyclists and horse riders also use it frequently. It follows the route of a disused railway line and was opened by David Bellamy.

There are several country houses which are open to the public in the Macclesfield area, including Addington Hall, which lies to the north. Mainly C15th, it has a Regency south front. It is half timbered, very lovely and set in fine grounds. The great hall is very interesting and the Georgian barn is now a tea room.

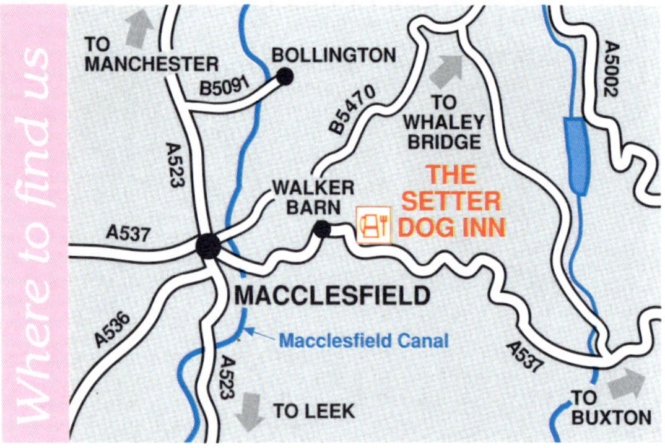


Should you prefer something stronger, the Setter Dog Inn at Walker Barn on the A537, some 3 miles east of Macclesfield is just the very spot.

Sited at 353 metres (1,158ft) above sea level, this friendly pub, which was also the local post office, is a particular favourite with people out sledging in winter and those magnificent maniacs in their four wheel drive machines who relish rallies in heavy snow conditions.

The Setter Dog Inn is open daily between 11.30am and 3pm and from 5.30pm until 11pm.

This is a very discreet pub: even the owner's name is Smith! And the head chef, Bob Pott, was previously with top Scottish hotel and restaurant, so should you desire a haggis he'll be happy to oblige.

Families are made welcome in the restaurant and the à la carte menu provides a wide selection of mouth watering dishes to choose from, all at reasonable prices.

There is a large car park and barbecues are held on summer weekends - why not try the deep-fried ice cream; rare, medium or well done?

**For further information, contact:**

**SETTER DOG INN,**
**WALKER BARN,**
**BUXTON ROAD, MACCLESFIELD,**
**CHESHIRE, SK11 OAW**
**TEL: 01625 431444**